Soviet Submarine Operations in Swedish Waters

THE WASHINGTON PAPERS

... intended to meet the need for an authoritative, yet prompt, public appraisal of the major developments in world affairs.

Series Editors: Walter Laqueur; Amos A. Jordan

Associate Editors: William J. Taylor, Jr.; Thomas Bleha

Executive Editor: Jean C. Newsom

Managing Editor: Nancy B. Eddy

Editorial Assistant: Christine L. Zibas

President, CSIS: Amos A. Jordan

MANUSCRIPT SUBMISSION

The Washington Papers and Praeger Publishers welcome inquiries concerning manuscript submissions. Please include with your inquiry a curriculum vitae, synopsis, table of contents, and estimated manuscript length. Manuscripts must be between 120–200 double-spaced typed pages. All submissions will be peer reviewed. Submissions to *The Washington Papers* should be sent to *The Washington Papers*; The Center for Strategic and International Studies; 1800 K Street NW; Suite 400; Washington, DC 20006. Book proposals should be sent to Praeger Publishers; One Madison Avenue; New York NY 10010.

The Washington Papers/128

Soviet Submarine Operations in Swedish Waters

1980–1986

Milton Leitenberg

Foreword by

Lawrence Freedman

Published with The Center for
Strategic and International Studies
Washington, D.C.

PRAEGER

New York
Westport, Connecticut
London

Library of Congress Cataloging-in-Publication Data

Leitenberg, Milton.
  Soviet submarine operations in Swedish waters, 1980–
1986.

  (The Washington papers, ISSN 0278-937X ; vol XIV, no. 128)
  "Published with the Center for Strategic and
International Studies, Washington, D.C."
  "Praeger special studies. Praeger scientific."
  Bibliography: p.
  Includes index.
  1. Sweden – Defenses.   2. Submarine boats – Soviet
Union.   3. Soviet Union – Military relations – Sweden.
4. Sweden – Military relations – Soviet Union.   I. Center
for Strategic and International Studies (Washington,
D.C.)   II. Title. III. Series.
VA593.L45   1987   359'.03'09485   87-13216
ISBN 0-275-92841-1 (alk. paper)
ISBN 0-275-92842-X (pbk. : alk. paper)

Library of Congress Catalog Card Number: 87–13216
ISBN: 0-275-92841-1 (cloth)
       0-275-92842-X (paper)

First published in 1987

Praeger Publishers, One Madison Avenue, New York, NY 10010
A division of Greenwood Press, Inc.

Printed in the United States of America

The paper used in this book complies with the Permanent
Paper Standard issued by the National Information Standards
Organization (Z39.48-1984).

10   9   8   7   6   5   4   3   2

Contents

Foreword

When on October 27, 1981 a Soviet Whiskey-Class submarine made a surprise appearance at Torumskär, 16 miles within one of the two most important Swedish naval base areas, well into Swedish internal waters, it captured international attention. The incident did undoubted damage to the reputation of the Soviet Union, and this damage was compounded when it was revealed that the submarine was carrying nuclear weapons. At a time when Moscow was waging a ferocious propaganda campaign against an increased U.S. nuclear presence in Europe, its own nuclear activities were brought into focus. Moreover, the victim was Sweden, a country whose neutralist status was envied by many in the West European peace movement.

For those who assumed that the Soviet Union was a perfectly decent neighbor unless unjustly provoked, the affair came as a shock. The "Whiskey-on-the-Rocks" incident might have been dismissed as an unfortunate aberration: perhaps some technical malfunction may have led it astray. It was soon revealed, however, to be part of a regular pattern of Soviet incursion into Swedish waters. More seriously, these incursions continued—indeed were stepped up—after this incident, and this continued violation of Swedish sovereignty was backed up by blatant lies, some of which were told at the highest level. The more Sweden protested, the more it was told it was inflicting damage on Soviet-Swedish relations. The more the Swedish navy sought to find and force to the surface the offending submarines, the more it risked accusations of provoking a major crisis.

While all this reflected badly on the Soviet Union, it posed considerable difficulties for Sweden. The Social Democratic government, which returned to office in October 1982, was acutely embarrassed by the continuing evidence of Soviet violations of its internal waters, for they were in a sense a violation of its most noble aspirations: that so long as Sweden strictly followed the principle of neutrality itself, the major powers would in turn respect Swedish neutrality with comparable rigour.

Milton Leitenberg provides in these pages a description that is at times almost painful — of a government caught between how things really were and how it wanted them to be. In practice it could not bring itself to follow through the logic of its declared policies because it feared the consequences of a confrontation with the Soviet Union. Leitenberg raises some disturbing questions with regard to the actual rules of engagement as compared to the more robust political statements under which the Swedish navy was allowed to seek out the intruders.

Why the Soviet Union chose to embarrass Sweden in this way remains something of a mystery. Straightforward political intimidation does not appear to be the primary motive, although it appears to be important in Moscow not to give way in disputes such as this however untenable its position in principle. After sifting through the various theories, Leitenberg suggests that the basic inspiration was operational. The Soviet Union views the Baltic as virtually a home sea and is anxious to secure control in war. In seeking to control all coastal areas it would be prepared to ensure that Sweden could not interfere in any way with its military effort. The submarine intrusions reflect the planning for this contingency. The timing may have been affected by a shift in operational doctrine and possibly concern over the military implications of the upheavals in Poland in the early 1980s.

This account of the regular penetration of Sweden's internal waters by Soviet submarines stands out in two ways. First, there is the meticulous and full presentation of the available evidence. This is a characteristic of Leitenberg's work and ensures that even those who do not accept his analysis will find this to be a valuable work of reference.

Second, there is a healthy intolerance of self-deception. Leitenberg is scathing when it comes to attempts to dismiss the intrusions as figments of the Swedish navy's imagination. The evidence — such as tracks of midget submarines close to the most sensitive naval facilities — is too damning. These were not "budget submarines," contrived threats designed to help the Swedish military's case for more resources, but a real reflection of Soviet policy.

Leitenberg's record is such that no one can dismiss him as an anti-Soviet propagandist. One of the benefits of a free society is that academics and other commentators can be irresponsible in the best sense of the word by bringing to the surface unpalatable truths and drawing awkward conclusions. The great value of this book is that it leaves us not only better informed but also less comfortable.

Lawrence Freedman
Professor
Department of War Studies
King's College London

About the Author

Milton Leitenberg, an analyst of defense policy and arms control issues, was a visiting research associate at the Swedish Institute of International Affairs from 1979 to 1987. Previously at the Center for International Studies at Cornell University and the Stockholm International Peace Research Institute (SIPRI), he has edited several volumes and written some 100 papers and monographs since beginning work in arms control and strategic studies in 1966. Among his books are the major portion of *Tactical Nuclear Weapons, European Perspectives,* SIPRI (Taylor & Francis, 1978), *Great Power Intervention in the Middle East* (co-edited, Pergamon Press, 1979), *The Structure of the Defense Industry: An International Survey* (coedited, Croom Helm, 1983), and *The Wars in Vietnam, Cambodia, and Laos, 1945–1982, A Bibliographic Guide* (coauthored, ABC-Clio, 1984). A book of selected studies on arms control, *Rüstung und Sicherheitspolitik,* was published in 1985 by Nomos Verlag, and a volume on *Military Research and Development* will be published by Croom Helm in 1988. The views expressed in this paper are solely those of the author.

Soviet Submarine Operations in Swedish Waters

Introduction

Even a neutral has a right to take account of facts. Even a neutral cannot be asked to close his mind or to close his conscience.
— Franklin Delano Roosevelt, 1939

Between 1980 and 1986 a continuous series of operations were carried out by foreign submarines deep in Swedish internal waters, often in restricted security zones adjacent to Sweden's major naval bases and in the vicinity of the nation's capital. On two occasions the submarines were officially identified as belonging to the USSR and, by strong implication, Soviet responsibility was attributed to the incidents that took place in 1980, 1981, and 1982. It is assumed that the Soviet navy was responsible for the submarine incursions in all but one or two of the other incidents as well. These incursions have continued despite public notes of protest from the Swedish government to the USSR, as well as private messages of protest from the Swedish prime minister. These submarine operations appear to be unique events in the post-World War II period: Sweden is a neutral state and not a member of any military alliance.[1]

This study deals with the issues of defense prepared-
ness, threat perception, and political responses. It exam-
ines how a country dealt with – or did not deal with – problems that it may not have anticipated, and may have had no
particular reason to anticipate, when its own preconcep-
tions and the norms of international behavior were clearly
contradicted by reality. It is a study that goes to the heart
of two words that Swedish political leaders have made the
touchstone of their national security policy of armed neutrality: *capability* and *will*.

Sweden records annual rates of incursions across its
borders and territorial waters in three categories: surface
vessels, aircraft, and submarines. Violations in the two non-
submarine classes are considered far less serious because
they cannot be covert, and the nation responsible can usually be easily and quickly identified and the intruder warned
off. The air incursions in particular tend to be brief, often
measured in seconds. The submarine violations, however,
must be considered deliberate.

The pattern of submarine incursions from 1980 onward
has been of a markedly different quality than those that
took place before that time in the character of the operations, their intensity (total number and frequency), and the
political context in which they have taken place. The political context is a direct consequence of the character of the
operations and the fact that they did not stop. An important portion of the description of these events therefore also
necessarily includes the responses of the Swedish government, both during and between the submarine incursions,
in addition to the description of the submarine operations
themselves. Before looking at the post-1980 events, we will
review the importance of the Baltic area and then look at
the incidence of roughly similar events in other countries,
particularly Sweden's Scandinavian neighbor Norway, a
member of NATO, and at the "background rate" of submarine violations recorded by Sweden.

*   *   *

Courtesy of Swedish National Defence Research Institute

The Baltic is an area that receives little attention in Western defense considerations. The southern tip of Sweden lies directly across the Baltic from the border between Poland and the German Democratic Republic (GDR)—a fact that is seldom recognized. The "East-West"—or North Atlantic Treaty Organization (NATO)/Warsaw Treaty Organization (WTO)—border is farther to the west. Before World War II, the USSR occupied fewer than 75 miles of the Baltic coast. It now incorporates well over half the distance from the Finnish border to West Germany, and its allies, Poland and the GDR, occupy the remainder. In other words, the USSR controls the entire southern coast of the Baltic from the Gulf of Finland to West Germany. Finland and Sweden share the northern Baltic shorelines. Sweden is the only immediate neighbor of the USSR bordering on the Baltic Sea that was not invaded by the USSR during World War II.

After World War II, the political alignments of the Scandinavian states and of the Central European countries bordering the Baltic to the south developed as follows:

• Norway, Denmark, Iceland, and West Germany have been members of NATO since 1949.
• Sweden has maintained a policy of neutrality.
• Finland's relations with the USSR have been governed by their 1948 Treaty of Friendship, Cooperation, and Mutual Assistance (FCMA).[2]

One routinely finds the phrase "the Nordic balance" used in the course of security policy discussions in the Nordic countries. This term does not refer to a military balance in its more traditional sense of a particular reckoning of military forces. Rather it is an ambiguous phrase indicating the varying political alignments of the participating nations moving geographically from west to east: Norway and Denmark in NATO, Sweden neutral, and Finland more closely associated with the USSR via the FCMA treaty.

The phrase is also used to denote the desirability of maintaining the status quo regarding both the political relationships and the specific military capabilities of the participating Nordic countries, whatever they happen to be at the moment. The limited Soviet political control of Finnish foreign and security policy is balanced by limited Danish and Norwegian participation in NATO: no allied bases, forces, or nuclear weapons on Danish or Norwegian territory in peacetime. A strongly armed Sweden that neither side wishes to see fall into the camp of the other side is situated in the middle. In more recent years, the phrase Nordic balance has increasingly been replaced by "Nordic stability," because the interest of the states in the region is to reduce images of power and counterpower, pressure and counterpressure, which could entail continuous dynamic changes.

The Baltic is a shallow sea of low salt content containing several large islands: Bornholm (Denmark), Öland and Gotland (Sweden), Ösel and Dagö (USSR), Rügen (GDR), and Åland (Finland). There are two large systems of archipelago islands, Finland-Åland and the Stockholm archipelago, and three large projections of the sea, the Gulfs of Bothnia, Finland, and Riga. One narrow passage between Sweden and Denmark – the Sound – and two within Danish territorial waters – the Great and Little Belts – separate the Baltic from the North Sea. The White Sea canal, which lies within the USSR, connects the Baltic with the White Sea, but is closed by ice some 200 days of the year.

Since World War II, Soviet Law of the Sea experts have categorized seas in three groups: internal seas, closed seas, and open seas. Historically, the USSR has considered the Baltic a "closed sea," as it does the Black Sea, and it continues to attempt to maintain this interpretation. The USSR uses this term to mean that the sea should be open to the merchant ships of all states, but that it should be closed both in peace and war to the military vessels of all states not bordering on the Baltic.[3] This would permit the navies of Finland, the USSR, Poland, the GDR, the Federal Re-

public of Germany (FRG), Denmark, and Sweden to operate
in the Baltic – as they currently all do – but no others. Sweden has always opposed this position and has maintained
the right of the military vessels of all states to enter the
Baltic. This is the situation that now exists. Ships of the
U.S. and British navies, for example, routinely enter the
Baltic.

On his trip to Finland, June 7–14, 1957, Soviet General
Secretary Nikita Khrushchev promoted the idea of the
"neutralization of the Baltic," and one week later the idea
was picked up in a joint statement of Poland and the GDR.
The USSR, in relation to this concept, began referring to
the Baltic as a "Sea of Peace" in the late 1950s. As early as
January 1945, a Soviet foreign ministry official had informed the representative of the Danish resistance movement in Moscow that the USSR "did not want to tolerate
any competition in the Baltic in the future."[4] Following the
failure of the Soviet Union to prevent Norway and Denmark
from joining NATO, one can see a progression of Soviet
proposals, first for the "neutralization of the Baltic" and
then for a Nordic Nuclear-Free Zone.

In the immediate postwar years and through the mid-
1950s the Baltic Fleet was the largest of the four fleets
maintained by the Soviet navy. Once the USSR began to
rebuild its naval forces in the 1950s and 1960s and to develop a truly oceangoing navy, however, it began to move its
major naval assets from the Baltic to the Kola Peninsula,
and the Baltic Fleet rapidly diminished in relative numbers
and in importance. The Northern Fleet, based on the Kola
Peninsula, and the Pacific Fleet became the most important
of the Soviet fleets. In the last 15 years the Soviet Baltic
Fleet has not increased significantly in strength, with one
exception. In 1976, at the height of détente and one year
after the 1975 Helsinki Accords, the USSR transferred six
older Golf-class nuclear-powered ballistic missile submarines (SSBNs) from service with the Northern Fleet and
permanently deployed them with the Baltic Fleet. One of
these submarines is kept on patrol in the Baltic at all times.

The USSR maintains more than half of its naval shipyard capacity for construction and repair in the Baltic, and new Soviet vessels often have their fitting-out trials in the Baltic. The USSR also carries out its major landing exercises in the Baltic. Both of these practices induce a substantial degree of concomitant Western and Swedish surveillance.

The traditional strategic notion regarding the Baltic has been that the Soviet Baltic Fleet would attempt to exit into the Atlantic in time of war and that Denmark and the narrow straits would be crucial in preventing this. More recently, a contrary interpretation is gaining increasing acceptance: the mission of the Soviet Baltic Fleet is not to exit the Baltic but to remain there to keep the NATO navies out and to assure the ability of the USSR to control the Baltic for Soviet military purposes without any external interference.

Phrased most generally, Swedish foreign policy toward the USSR was formulated in the early postwar years by Foreign Minister Östen Undén, and its essential character was to be on as good terms with the USSR as possible and not gratuitously to irritate its more powerful neighbor. The only outstanding diplomatic issue between Sweden and the USSR — aside from the subject of this study — has been the delineation of the disputed maritime boundary in the Baltic between the Soviet coast and the Swedish mid-Baltic island of Gotland. Negotiations regarding this issue have been in progress since 1969.

1

The Overall Incidence of Violations: 1970–1986

Sweden has published records of foreign submarine violations of its internal and territorial waters since 1962. It classifies these events into three groups: (a) violation, including probable violations; (b) possible violation; and, in some years, (c) other incidents. The same three groupings are used for classifying air incursions. For sea surface incursions, "other incidents" is replaced by "transit without prior notification." Using these designations, Swedish defense authorities have released the figures shown in table 1.[1]

The submarine violations—as distinguished from maritime incursions on the surface and those in the air—are considered particularly significant for Swedish national security considerations because they must be assumed to be purposeful in the great majority of cases. Sweden also maintains data on those incidents that are caused by ships or aircraft of NATO member states and those by WTO members, particularly in the air and sea-surface categories. These disaggregations have only been released more recently, for example in the reports for the years 1984 and 1985. Air incursions are known to be made much more often by aircraft of various NATO member states than they are by WTO aircraft. The air incursions for which NATO is respon-

TABLE 1
Incidence of Violations in Internal and
Territorial Waters (1970–1986)

| | Submarine: (Categories a,b,c)[1] | Sea Surface | | Air: (Category a) |
		Violations (Category a)	Without Prior Notice (Category c)	
1970	—[2]	9	—	12
1971	—	3	—	19
1972	—	2	—	23
1973	—	7	—	19
1974	—	8	—	15
1975	15	9	4	20
1976	10	11	11	21
1977	12	19	13	28
1978	5	5	5	25
1979	7	7	31	77
1980	11	13	44	50
1981	12	12	28	49
1982	52	30	42	28
1983[3] (a)	25	5	25	29
(c) "around 60"				
1984 (a) "around 20"		2	30	24
(c) "around 50"				
1985 (a) "around 15"		3	38	26
1986 (c) over 15				

1. Category (a) includes violations and probable violations, category (b) is possible violation, and category (c) is "other incidents."

2. Dashes indicate that the information is not available or was not publicly provided.

3. In 1983, 1984, 1985, and 1986, the submarine totals omitted category (b) as well as category (c), which they had always included in the past. I have therefore indicated what those values were, as provided by other sources such as Roger Magnergård, "Commander in Chief's Numbers for 1983: 25 Certain Violations of Sweden's Border," *Svenska Dagbladet*, June 28, 1984; Lars Christiansson, "Commander in Chief's Submarine Report: New Violations Interpreted Carefully, *Svenska Dagbladet*, January 31, 1983. Beginning in 1983, the accounting criteria for sea surface violations also appear to have been changed.

sible take place for the greatest part off the coast of southern Sweden (the province of Skåne) and just south of Oslo, Norway. Only on the rarest of occasions are the air incursions considered serious by Swedish authorities, and several more serious incidents in 1984 and 1985 were caused by Soviet aircraft.

In releasing another time-series of data in 1983 solely on submarine incursions, the report of the Swedish Submarine Defense Commission (SDC) omitted category (c), "other incidents," which produced slightly lower numbers.[2] (See tables 2 to 4.) For example, for the six years 1975 through 1980, the commission's tally results in 40 events versus 60 in the Defense staff account. More important, however, the Defense staff accountings for 1983 and 1984 suddenly omitted category (b) as well as category (c), which made an enormous difference: in two years alone, around 45 events versus some 110. An equally significant difference would have been noted in 1982 if the most certain category of events had been the only one counted.

It became clear in the course of this study, however, that the relation of these statistics to the number of submarine incursions that may have actually occurred is unknown. This was admitted in a Swedish parliamentary Defense Committee report released in May 1985:

> The circumstance that underwater incursions can be concealed *and are only occasionally detected* is the main reason why it is not possible to present exact statistics on these activities.[3] (Author's italics)

As early as April 1980, a Swedish naval officer had written that

> Our oversight of the underwater territorial sea is so poor that it must be considered a pure coincidence if we detect a foreign submarine there.[4]

TABLE 2
Annual Submarine Violations, 1962–1982

	Violations (including probable violations)	Possible violations	Total
1962	1	—	1
1963	3	—	3
1964	—	2	2
1965	—	—	—
1966	4	—	4
1967	—	8	8
1968	1	2	3
1969	4	5	9
1970	—	7	7
1971	1	2	3
1972	2	2	4
1973	—	2	2
1974	3	4	7
1975	3	6	9
1976	1	6	7
1977	2	6	8
1978	—	2	2
1979	1	4	5
1980	5	4	9
1981	4	6	10
1982	18	22	40
Total	53	90	143

Source: Report of the Submarine Defense Commission, 1983.

A report prepared by the conservative Moderate Party two years later stated that

> only a very small proportion of the violations that oc-
> cur are reported, and only a small fraction of those can
> in turn be verified, for example by an assured hy-

TABLE 3
Distribution of Submarine Violations over
Military Districts, 1962–1982

| | | *Distribution By Military District* | | | | | |
Incidents	*Number*	*Upper Norr-land*	*Lower Norr-land*	*East*	*South*	*West*	*Got-land*
Violations (including probable violations)	53	2	6	23	8	7	7
Possible violations	90	–	16	39	10	14	11
Total	143	2	22	62	18	21	18

Source: Report of the Submarine Defense Commission, 1983.

TABLE 4
Submarine Violations of Internal Waters and
Territorial Sea, 1962–1982

Incidents	*Number*	*Internal Waters*	*Territorial Sea*
Violations (including probable violations)	53	29	24
Possible violations	90	45	45
Total	143	74	69

Source: Report of the Submarine Defense Commission, 1983.

drophone contact from an ASW [antisubmarine warfare] equipped helicopter or ship . . . A large portion of the violations that have been assuredly established, and which led to the use of warning munitions or depth charges, have been detected by naval units or ASW helicopters that were out on routine patrol. In many cases helicopters have found submarines by pure coincidence during maneuvers.[5]

This pattern continued as late as 1984 and 1985 when Swedish forces "stumbled over foreign submarines during maneuvers."[6] In November 1985 the second most senior officer in the Swedish navy stated that "the chances of detecting a foreign submarine in our waters today are very low — less than one percent."[7] In addition, the shifting of category definitions as well as the use of ambiguous phrasing in the most recent annual reports passed virtually without public notice.

Border violation statistics of the type that were publicized up to 1983 are no longer publicly available. The difficulties of exactly classifying different indications has been given as the primary reason for this change. The system of quarterly reports on violations has shown certain deficiencies in the past year. The phrasing has displayed a hackneyed emptiness particularly as regards the underwater submarine violations.[8]

Chronology

Major Violations	Directly Related Political Events
1. Utö-Huvudskär, September 18–October 9, 1980	
2. U-137 stranding, Karlskrona, October 1981	• Swedish protest note to the USSR; rejected by USSR. Nonsocialist government

(continued)

Chronology (*continued*)

Major Violations	Directly Related Political Events
	postpones all ministerial level exchanges with the USSR.
3. Hårsfjärden area, Muskö Naval Base, October–November 1982.	• Submarine Defense Commission empaneled, November 1982.
	• Commission report released and protest note to the USSR, April 26, 1983.
4. Sundsvall (and Hardangerfjord, Norway), May 1983.	• USSR rejects Swedish protest, May 1983. Personal message from Swedish Prime Minister Palme to Soviet leadership, May 1983. The Palme government decides to maintain halt on ministerial level exchanges with the USSR.
5. Töre, etc., July 1983.	
6. Karlskrona, August–September 1983.	
7. Divers at mine chain; North Stockholm archipelago, September 1983.	• Partial disclosure of Prime Minister's message, December 1983.
	• Swedish government decides prior to Soviet Foreign Minister Gromyko's visit to the Stockholm Conference on Security and Confidence Building Measures and to meet with Palme to renew high-level diplomatic exchanges with the USSR, January 1984.

(continued)

Chronology (*continued*)

Major Violations	Directly Related Political Events
	• USSR Foreign Minister Gromyko at opening of Stockholm Conference and meets with Prime Minister Palme, mid-January 1984.
8. Karlskrona Naval Base, February–March 1984.	• Sweden informs the USSR during the Karlskrona ASW operations that ministerial level exchanges will take place.
	• Disclosure of actual nature of Palme-Gromyko discussions, April 6–7, 1984.
9. Major Soviet aircraft violation over Gotland, August 1984.	• Sweden protests aircraft violation after the event is publicly leaked. USSR rejects protest. Protest repeated; rejection repeated.
10. Continued submarine violations in 1984 and 1985, particularly in October 1985 near Stockholm following the Swedish national elections. Soviet aircraft violation over Gotland again, June 1985.	• Euphemistic government statement following elections, and Prime Minister Palme's trip to Moscow set for April 1986. Swedish naval officers protest the government's ASW policy.

2

Analogous Events in Other Countries

More or less routine Soviet submarine operations take place close to French and British ballistic missile submarine bases, as well as particular NATO naval bases such as La Spezia (Italy), or, up to the withdrawal of U.S. ballistic missile submarines in 1979, Rota (Spain), and the Azores area. In these instances, Soviet submarines typically stay in international waters, and their function is well understood. These operations are not discussed in this paper.

Japan

On August 25, 1983, Japanese sources reported that tracks had been found on the sea bottom in the Tsugaru Strait between Honshu and Hokkaido and that naval divers were seeking a midget submarine suspected of having made them.[1] It was a rare instance in which this kind of activity had been publicly reported in Japan, despite the fact that similar submarine operations had been taking place for some time and were known to the Japanese government and even to members of the press.[2] Tracks of bottom-crawling vehicles, similar to those found in Sweden's Hårsfjärden in 1982, were described as being so dense in some areas that the sea bottom "looked like a barnyard that had been criss-crossed by tractors."[3] In August 1985, Japanese government authorities released a diagram of an 180-meter-long stretch of bottom-markings left by a tracked midget submarine after investigations in the Tsugaru and Soya (or La Pérouse) Straits (and apparently in the Korea Strait as well) and reported that "Soviet special forces had operated in Japanese waters."[4] In the fall of 1984, it was reported that Swedish defense authorities had compared the bottom tracks found in Swedish waters with those found in Japan.[5]

Italy

On February 24, 1982, a nuclear powered submarine, assumed to be a Soviet Victor-class nuclear powered attack submarine (SSN), intruded into Italian territorial waters southeast of Taranto. The submarine was chased for 18 hours by Italian aircraft, helicopters, and naval vessels. The Italian Foreign Ministry issued a protest, which did not name the USSR as the intruder, but announced that the Soviet ambassador had been called to the ministry and broadly hinted that the summons was in relation to the submarine incident.[6]

Denmark/Greenland

On July 13, 1983, a submarine surfaced about 25 meters from the boat of a local official in Disko Bay on Greenland's west coast. The location, Egedesminde, is far inside Greenland's internal waters – not a place that a submarine would reach by navigational error. An editorial in the principal Danish daily newspaper explicitly referred to the submarine as "a Soviet submarine."[7] The incident occurred just as a Nordic peace festival was taking place in Denmark.

In a different practice, which also produced disturbing political consequences for Denmark, the USSR carried out

large-scale landing exercises on the flat and sandy Mecklen-
burg coast of the GDR in June and September 1980, not far
from the similarly flat and sandy Danish coast.[8] These land-
sea maneuvers were previously held in the Gulf of Finland,
and they have gradually moved westward, closer to the
Danish and West German borders.[9] They have also had an
important military consequence: tactical warning time for
Denmark has been reduced from three to four hours to 15
minutes. In 1978, Danish authorities also reported that Soviet aircraft violated Danish air space about once a month.[10]

Norway

The largest number of events aside from Sweden itself —
although of a more varied character — have taken place in
Norway, Sweden's neighbor. In regard to overall numbers,
Norwegian authorities have released two sets of figures for
submarine incursions. The first of these reported 226 "observations of submarines" between 1969 and 1982.[11] These
"observations" include a null class, however: those subsequently classified as certainly negative, or no submarine,
which accounted for 104 of the 226 observations. (In addition, 29 of the total of 226 were from a single event in
Sognefjord in 1972.) The remaining 122 in the 13-year period are divided into three categories: "definite submarine,
probable (or likely) submarine, and possible submarine."
The numbers given for these are "a handful" — quoted elsewhere as 4 to 5 — of definite submarines, 10 to 20 probable
submarines, and the remainder, possible. At the same time,
the description of the repeated sonar contacts obtained by
two Norwegian surface vessels and an Orion aircraft in the
submarine hunt in Andsfjord off Andöy Island on June 30,
1983, which was classified as "possible submarine, grade
4" — the highest likelihood category in the possible submarine grouping — suggests that a large portion of the possi-
bles — and therefore even more likely all of the probables —
should be assumed to have been definite identifications.[12] If

this suggestion is correct, it would bring the total up to perhaps 40 in the period from 1969 to the present. The second set of data was published in the Norwegian government's report of the 1983 Hardangerfjord events discussed below. In this compilation, 175 observations are reported for the period 1969 to May 1983, with 75 in the "no submarine" class. The remaining 100 observations are reported as 3 definite submarines, 12 probable, and 85 possible.[13] The comments above regarding what seems a more likely redistribution among these categories would apply to the second set of figures as well.

Norwegian naval authorities indicate that "in the most recent years" the number of observations (which must include the null class) have averaged about 20 per year. The Norwegian statistics reportedly show large annual variations with a noticeable rise since 1979. Oddly enough, the largest concentration of definite and probable observations is reported as having taken place in the earlier half of the period, with peaks in 1972 and in 1975. This timing is explained by a sharpening in the rules of Norwegian naval response to suspected submarine violations, which went into effect in January 1976. The geographical distribution of the observations falls primarily into four areas: Hardangerfjord, just southeast of Bergen; Sognefjord; the Tysfjord-Ofotfjord-Vestfjord group, near Narvik; and partly also the fjords in the Finnmark areas.

The most well-known submarine incursions in Norwegian waters took place in Sognefjord in November 1972 and in Hardangerfjord from April 27 to May 6, 1983. The 1983 Hardanger events began exactly 24 hours after the Swedish SDC released its public report in Stockholm, and, as the operation continued, it overlapped with a major submarine operation that was taking place in Sweden. Norway has never officially identified the state to which the submarines belong, claiming that motor sound recordings were absent. Norwegian naval officers have implied unofficially at various times, however, that they could only be Warsaw Pact vessels, which in practice means the USSR or Poland. Early in 1986, the Norwegian commander in chief was somewhat more explicit:

> We have evidence to say that this is a tactic and technique used by the Warsaw Pact without my commenting on its magnitude. We have after all seen the Soviet Union consciously violate territorial waters here in the Scandinavian area.[14]

The Hardangerfjord submarine was allegedly a diesel-powered vessel and, from a reported 30-minute visual identification, was suspected of being a Whisky-class submarine. Within a single 24-hour period in the submarine hunt, 24 Terne ASW rockets and several depth charges were used, including two dropped from an Orion aircraft. Soon after these ASW operations, a Norwegian military officer was quoted as publicly stating that the Norwegian navy "could have destroyed Soviet submarines that . . . enter[ed] territorial waters this spring, but chose not to do so for political reasons." Government directions to the Norwegian navy had been only to force the submarine to the surface: "It is a tough decision. . . . It is still peacetime, and you can't really destroy a submarine. . . . it is not an attack on Norwegian soil."[15] The Norwegian submarine commission report that reviewed the Hardangerfjord case criticized the command of the submarine hunt, however, and, as in the Swedish submarine commission report, the quality of the ASW equipment that was available on board the Norwegian ships. By coincidence, some 10 ships of NATO's Standing Naval Force Atlantic (STANAVFORLANT) were only a few miles away in Bergen harbor all during this submarine hunt and could easily have supplied helicopter as well as other additional ASW support. Nevertheless, Norwegian authorities decided that only national forces should be used. It was additionally decided not to exclude civilian shipping from the area, although doing so would have facilitated the search for a submarine.

Submarine sightings and searches in the area of Hardangerfjord have been reported in November 1970, May

1974, August 1977, November 1980, January and April 1983, and another in Sognefjord in March 1976.[16] There were three or four additional submarine sightings early in 1983 within Norwegian territorial waters followed by the one already referred to near Andöy Island in June 30, 1983. This was presumably the same Soviet Foxtrot-class submarine that only a few days previously had appeared on the surface together with two Soviet electronic intelligence (Elint) vessels directly alongside a Norwegian vessel making seismic observations in international waters near Tromsö. Another event took place on February 20–23, 1984 in Tysfjord. Depth charges were used, but the event was nevertheless only classified as a "probable" submarine. The most recent event reported took place in Sognefjord in May–June 1985 and involved three Norwegian Orion aircraft and several surface ships in the ASW operations. The Norwegian government has never claimed to have found bottom tracks or referred to midget submarine operations in its waters.[17]

Norwegian authorities state that there have been only eight incursions by Soviet aircraft over Norwegian territory since 1976.[18] This number is low in contrast to Sweden, where there may be nearly that many per year by Soviet aircraft (seven in 1984, three in 1985). There is one other series of extremely unusual – virtually bizarre – incursions by Soviet ships, and in this case they were unquestionably Soviet ships, into Norwegian territorial waters. They were civilian surface vessels.

In the brief period between June 18 and August 13, 1978, no fewer than 16 violations of Norwegian territorial waters by Soviet surface vessels took place – and 12 of them in the 30 days between June 27 and July 28. Nearly all were in a relatively restricted portion of the northernmost Norwegian coast from the North Cape eastward to the Soviet border.[19] This was a substantially higher rate of such events than the normal background rate.[20] No submarines or other Soviet military vessels were involved. All the ships were civilian: tugboats, lumber carriers, freighters, research vessels, and one East German ship. All came within Norwegian territorial waters; many cut engines and anchored as well. Those who were questioned uniformly supplied dubious explanations: bad weather when the weather was good, ill seamen, engine trouble; but the ships then steamed off as Norwegian naval vessels approached. None of the Soviet ships made any attempt to conceal themselves – it was in fact the season of the midnight sun and detection was more or less unavoidable, particularly because many of the Soviet vessels seem to have remained at anchor until approached. The official Soviet explanation offered was totally unconvincing: that in most of the cases the ships had simply been in "innocent passage."

A Norwegian researcher who posed questions about these events to senior foreign-policy researchers in Moscow was treated to laughter by way of reply, and denials "that the USSR would do anything so stupid". A Soviet apology was made for one of the 16 incidents.

The official Norwegian government response was as inexplicable as were the Soviet explanations. Early in July, as the events began, official Norwegian statements clearly presented the incursions as provocative and purposeful. But suddenly all the incidents were officially attributed to coincidence and normal boat traffic – though they had not occurred with that frequency and in that area previously. The extreme implausibility of the Norwegian government's explanation was further made embarrassingly plain when the incidents ended as suddenly as they had begun. Suggestions as to the possible purpose of the submarine incursions in Norwegian internal waters – presumably Soviet – will be discussed later, together with those in Swedish waters, but whatever the purpose of the incursions by Soviet surface vessels, it is important to point out that they took place in mid-1978, before the serious deterioration of the supposed U.S.-USSR/East-West détente period. The next such publicly reported incident took place in November 1982, when a Soviet icebreaker was discovered in a Norwegian military area near the island of Fuglö north of Tromsö. The Norwegian Foreign Ministry filed a formal protest with the USSR.[21]

Finland

In June 1982, a Finnish coast guard vessel dropped warning charges on a submerged submarine in Finnish internal waters in the Åland archipelago.[22] Finnish officials make much of their claim that they handle this problem in a different way from that of Sweden. Finland does not disclose whether violations have taken place, and if they have, the Finnish naval or government response is not announced. It is therefore not possible to say whether violations of Finnish waters by submarines are taking place or not and, if they are, what their frequency is. Finnish authorities also claim that they have "better knowledge of what takes place under the surface of their waters than Sweden does thanks to an ingenious system of fixed hydrophones and magnetic detection facilities."[23]

The few public statements that are available from Finnish authorities are contradictory and ambiguous: In mid-1983 senior Finnish defense officials claimed that "no violations of Finnish territorial waters have been demonstrated," despite the record of the June 1982 event. Several days later, Finnish Foreign Minister Paavo Väyrynen admitted that Finland had been visited by a foreign submarine in the summer of 1982.[24] The very next day it was reported that Finnish coastal defense authorities were making observations in the Gulf of Finland, but would not indicate where these were, or whether the object being observed was in the air, on the sea surface, or underwater.[25] In 1985, Finnish officials anonymously indicated that "only a few not particularly serious (submarine) violations had been noticed in Finnish waters in recent years."[26]

The questions that are immediately posed are what the Finnish criteria are for such an event being "noticed" and within which government authority does that "notice" take place.

3

Events in Sweden

Two major alterations in Sweden's naval-force structure and in its coastal-defense capabilities in the 1970s undoubtedly played a substantial role in a combination of ways in the events that were to follow. They reduced Sweden's capability to detect submarine incursions, and they reduced Sweden's capability to deal with intruding submarines once they were present and detected in internal and territorial waters.

The major developments were the scrapping of three existing fixed hydrophone systems for the detection of intruding submarines and the demobilization of frigates and destroyers in the Swedish navy, which had or should have had the mission and equipment for ASW, without their replacement by new ships.

It is important to note that the primary mission of these vessels had not been antisubmarine warfare within internal waters and inside the archipelago. Nevertheless, they were the only available Swedish naval ships with the most closely appropriate equipment and would have been used for the purpose had the circumstances presented themselves.

In the early 1970s, allegedly on economic grounds, Sweden's coastal defense forces dismantled three bottom-mounted hydrophone systems that had been in use for some 15 years:

1. an "active hydrophone" or short-range sonar system that was used particularly in the vicinity of important naval security areas — just the locations in which many of the post-1980 submarine incursions took place;
2. a passive hydrophone system, of somewhat longer range, also located in Swedish naval security areas;
3. variable-depth hydrophone buoys that were also used for the collection of a catalogue of motor and propeller recordings of foreign submarines, an activity that reportedly had been started in the early 1970s by the Swedish defense agencies.[1]

Such recordings can provide a signature not only of submarine classes, but also of individual submarines. They can also distinguish the number of cylinders in a submarine diesel engine, as well as the number of propellers (one or two) that the submarine may have. For example, a crucial distinguishing characteristic of a Soviet Whisky-class submarine is that it contains a double screw and two propellers.

In 1972, the Swedish Parliament decided as part of its forthcoming five-year defense program that Sweden would no longer have surface vessels designated solely for anti-submarine warfare: these would be "strongly reduced or entirely abstained from."[2] This conscious and nearly unanimous decision meant that Sweden became the only coastal state in Europe to decide to do without ASW vessels. The Parliament decided that "the protection of commercial shipping should take place with other than military means": Sweden's neutrality policy and general foreign policy were to be the means of protecting its maritime transport. Sweden would instead put all its defense resources into building a capability to deter a land invasion. There had been a continuous reduction of capital ships in the Swedish navy since the end of World War II. (See tables 5 and 6.) The 1985 report of the commander in chief describing the changes

TABLE 5
Swedish Naval Forces, 1967–1987

	1967	1987
Surface attack vessels	57	34
Submarines	24	12
Mine clearing flotillas	14	8
Coastal artillery battalions	40	29

Source: Ministry of Defense (Sweden), *Commander in Chief 85, Perspective Plan, Part II*, October 1, 1985, p. 34.

between 1967 and 1987 indicates a reduction of naval forces of nearly 50 percent.

Personnel in the Swedish navy's peacetime organization dropped from 9,000 in 1965 to 7,900 in 1972, and to 7,000 in 1982, a reduction of 22 percent. Another 10 percent were still to be reduced after 1982. In the beginning of the 1970s there were still 14 ships – 8 destroyers and 6 frigates – that

TABLE 6
Development of the Wartime Organization, Swedish Naval Forces

Type of vessel	1955	1966	1977	1985	1989	1995
Battleships	2	—	—	—	—	—
Cruisers	3	1	—	—	—	—
Destroyers/Frigates	25	17	8	—	—	—
Torpedo/Missile/Patrol boats	40	34	34	34	34	34
Submarines	21	21	17	12	12	12
Minesweeping units	16	14	14	11	8	8
Coastal artillery battalions	43	41	34	30	30	30

Source: Erik Lidén, "Battle Within the Military About the Future of the Armed Forces," *Svenska Dagbladet*, July 23, 1985.

were equipped with ASW sonar. The government's defense decisions of 1968 and 1972 determined that these would be successively demobilized as they reached retirement age: all but one or two had been decommissioned by 1980.

At the time of the first major submarine event in 1980, which initiated the new pattern of events, only the destroyer *Halland*, which was normally assigned the role of command of torpedo boat attack vessels, was still able to participate. Nevertheless, it too was taken out of service in 1982. The navy's minesweepers and patrol boats were allegedly outfitted with only the most simple sonars and were neither intended nor suited for ASW. The entire ASW mission was delegated to seven heavy helicopters, which also performed other functions and whose numbers were not expected to increase through 1983–1984. A Swedish naval author has also listed two other secondary circumstances that he felt contributed to deficiencies in detecting intruding submarines: the reduction of the year-round population in the large archipelagos off the east-central Baltic coast of Sweden because of changes in structural employment patterns and the replacement of lighthouses.

It is reasonable to assume, as a result of all of these developments in the 1970s, that one effect was that fewer submarines were observed in Swedish territorial waters than may actually have been there. There may also have been another effect: these cumulative changes may have increased the willingness—marginally, or to a greater degree—of the USSR to carry out the submarine incursions. One is impressed not primarily with the difficulty of inshore ASW in the Baltic—although it is difficult, and it was the Swedish navy's continuous plaint in the early 1980s—but that the navy had little or no ASW.

Swedish defense authorities have recorded Elint signatures from foreign submarines in international waters in the Baltic.[3] They were also able to identify to some degree the land-based communications facilities that were utilized by Warsaw Pact submarines while in the Baltic, which has aided in identifying the class and national ownership of particular submarines. Only on the rarest of occasions have Swedish or Norwegian naval authorities ever made any public mention of communication intercepts or of engine-acoustic signature recordings. Either or both of these would help to resolve the question of the national allegiance of intruding submarines. Both Norway and Sweden are probably fully capable of making both of these types of recordings and possess identifying signature catalogues with which to match them. Norway would presumably have access to NATO-developed signature collections. A crucial aspect of the post-1982 developments in particular is the Swedish government's claim that it is unable to specify the nationality of the foreign submarines.

In June 1984, for the first time, the Swedish commander in chief released information regarding the interception of communications with the stranded Soviet Whisky-class submarine in the area of Karlskrona in October 1981. It was not until mid-1983 that either Swedish communications intelligence (Comint) or Elint capabilities were so much as mentioned in the Swedish media. Even then they were mentioned in no more than one or two newpapers, never in television reporting, and never in conjunction with an individual incident. At the time of the 1972 Sognefjord event in Norway, when the submarine involved was also suspected of being a Whisky-class vessel, the nationality of the submarine was considered an open question, at least in public discussion. Although participation of Polish Whisky-class submarines over the years in these incursions cannot be absolutely ruled out on the basis of existing public evidence, the degree to which the operations have been subsequently carried out, as well as the involvement of midget submarines, would suggest that Polish involvement is extremely unlikely and that these have been operations carried out by Soviet submarines alone.

Sweden maintains a 12-nautical-mile territorial boundary. The Swedish phrase "inre vatten" (inner or internal waters) is the area from the coastline to a line connecting the outer rocks and skerries, or base points. The 12-nautical-mile boundary is then reckoned from that line. For some time it was thought that the first submarine incursions in inner Swedish coastal waters did not take place until the late 1970s. Such events, however, were in fact on public record previously, though infrequently.

According to Swedish naval authorities, all of the interactions between Swedish naval vessels and unidentified submarines inside Swedish waters prior to 1980 had followed a common pattern. When visual or sonar contact was made with a submarine, warning munitions were used. Under international law, the submarine was to react immediately by shifting course so as to leave Swedish territorial waters. If this did not take place, munitions were to be used to force the submarines to leave. This sequence was to be repeated after each contact with the intruding submarine; that is, if contact with the submarine was lost and then regained, warning munitions were again to be used first even if the submarine had not changed course to take it out of Swedish waters. If munitions were used in peacetime for "effective fire," their purpose was to force the submarine to the surface, not to damage it seriously. In 1970 a Swedish naval source supplied a description of the effects of a full strength depth charge as light damage to submarine if detonated within 25 meters from "a modern submarine" and damage to submarine serious enough to sink it if detonated within 10 meters from the submarine.[4]

In 1980 this estimate was modified to detonation within 15 meters to produce light damage and within 5 meters to sink the submarine.[5] Because the margin between the two is extremely small and uncertainty about the submarine's location due to environmental impact on ASW search and location sensors can be as large — and there was no desire to sink a submarine — depth charges, when used, were dropped at sufficient distance from any presumed submarine to preclude the danger of damaging the submarine. The desire to avoid producing major damage also led to the Swedish emphasis in the early 1980s on the development of an "incident weapon" for use in peacetime.

As early as 1969, the commander of Sweden's coastal naval forces had recommended that the "Ordinance Containing Instructions for the Swedish Armed Forces in Times of Peace and in a State of Neutrality" (IKFN) regulations, which define the rules of engagement with intruding submarines for Swedish military forces in peacetime, be changed so that upon contact with a submarine within Swedish territorial waters operations should directly attempt to force the submarine to the surface. The recommendations were, however, not accepted. As will be seen, the IKFN regulations were modified in 1982 to include that recommendation for application in 1983, but only within internal waters. The new sequence can be described as follows: first warning shots; then use of depth charges "at a certain distance" from the submarine; then, in a third stage, depth charges with the purpose of forcing the submarine to come to the surface. It is clear, however, that depth charges have never been close enough to a submarine to damage it – no submarine has ever felt the necessity of surfacing under an attack – and in practice it is not known whether and when there has been any difference in the requirement of "a certain distance" in the second or third stages. The use of lower strength munitions of various sizes has also been frequent. It is difficult to ascertain exactly what practices have been followed because the available evidence indicates that practice has varied in different incidents both before and after the change in regulations in 1982–1983.

Incidents Prior to 1980

1962

Three Swedish destroyers, led by the *Halland*, waiting for a target in an antiaircraft exercise near the island of Fårö, north of Gotland, all registered a submarine periscope on radar, submarine propeller sound on hydrophone, and doppler response on active sonar. The submarine was attacked with depth charges and with antisubmarine rockets from each of the destroyers, "several hundred meters from the submarine," and was followed to the territorial boundary where the destroyers broke off the chase. The press and even some quarters of the navy were nevertheless skeptical of the report.[6]

1966

A submarine was sighted in Gullmarsfjord on the west coast. Navy staff officers were at first skeptical: navigation in the area is difficult, some of the reports come from relatively shallow areas, and "it is unlikely that many submarines would violate Swedish waters simultaneously."[7] Nevertheless, two small minesweepers dropped warning munitions, and then by using two 50 kilogram (kg) plumbs, made "mechanical contact" with an object at 15 meters depth in 30 meters of water. A coastal minesweeper dropped depth charges, and subsequent analysis provided convincing evidence of submarines, with the suspicion that some of the vessels were smaller than the size of a customary submarine. The press again expressed skepticism at the reports.

1969

A naval officer reported in September 1969 that "Once again a submarine has with the greatest likelihood appeared deep in Swedish territorial waters, and additionally within a prohibited security area."[8] There was no indication of Swedish naval response in this case.

The 1970s

In May 1974, an unidentified submarine was chased off Gotland. Depth charges were used. Between 1969 and 1979 submarine violations averaged around 7 to 8 per year according to the SDC report, and 11 to 13 per year from 1975–1979 according to the Defense figures. Every one of these events was met with skepticism in some quarters. There has never been a public statement regarding whether sonar signatures from ship, shore, or helicopter-borne sensors were recorded on film or tape in any of these events and have been permanently preserved. Those events that were reported in the press during these years gave rise to the expression "budget submarines," which not only meant disbelief that they were real submarines, but implied that false reports were being contrived by the military services to obtain increased budgetary allotments.

1980: A New Pattern

The first indication of a new pattern of events took place in an incident off the southeast coast of Sweden on March 12, 1980. A submarine was detected far inside territorial waters in the Blekinge archipelago at the entrance to Karlskrona, one of Sweden's two major naval bases. The submarine was sighted by a minesweeper when the destroyer *Halland* was again relatively close by. The submarine dove after warning munitions were dropped, but water conditions were excellent (isothermal) for sonar, and the sonar registered both propeller sound and doppler effect. The submarine steered south, away from the coast, to the territorial boundary line. It stopped there and began to use its own active sonar to locate the Swedish vessel and then turned north to travel back into Swedish waters once again. A full strength depth charge was now dropped, but again as warning — that is, sufficiently distant from the submarine so as to avoid damage. The commander of the Karlskrona naval base specifically ordered the *Halland's* captain *not* to use "effective fire."[9] There was no public reaction by military or government authorities or press attention.

The incident that followed six months later was the first that received extensive public attention and is usually described as beginnning the new pattern of interaction between the intruding submarines and Swedish ships. On September 18, 1980, an unidentified submarine was discovered in the vicinity of the islands of Utö and Huvudskär in the southern Stockholm archipelago, quite close to Sweden's main naval base at Muskö in Hårsfjärden. These were the locations that were to figure again so prominently in the events of the fall of 1982. According to Swedish naval sources, a portion of the submarine's conning tower with raised mast and antennae was observed by a naval tugboat, and if the submarine had not been "observed by the naked eye, it would not have been detected."[10] A submarine hunt then began, again led by the *Halland*, which lasted from September 18 to 30 and demonstrated many of the characteristics of the kinds of interactions that followed for the next five years.

• Instead of turning out to international waters, the submarine stays within Swedish internal waters, possibly even coming closer to the coast and makes no effort to "escape," that is, to leave.
• It then, in essence, exercises ASW operations with Swedish naval forces for an extended period of days or weeks. In this case, it stayed for two weeks. Visual and hydrophone contacts were reported until September 30, and at times the "submarine could be followed for a relatively long period."[11]
• Simultaneously, one or more foreign submarines are initially in the same general area within Swedish territorial waters or additional submarines may either come into the area while the ASW operations are under way or approach just to the edge of Swedish territorial waters in the vicinity. In the 1980 case a second submarine was detected close to the first during the ASW operations.
• The captain of the *Halland* reported that "commanders of the ships engaging in the ASW operations were ordered to be careful even at the stage of using warning muni-

tions, and not to use 'effective fire' in any manner without specific orders"[12] and that "The Commander-in-Chief forbade the engaged units from following the IKFN regulations and to use effective fire only on his personal order."[13] In earlier years the purpose of the ASW operations was to turn the submarine out into international waters. In later years it was to force the submarine to the surface, but not to do so by intentionally attempting to damage it. Not before September 28, 10 days after the operations began and after repeated evasive maneuvers by the still present submarines, was effective fire used, "as near as the weapons' precision allowed without aiming for a hit."[14]

• Sizable Swedish forces are sent in, both ships and helicopters. Munitions expenditure may seem sizable, but is not intended to damage or sink the submarine. In this case, after the use of warning munitions, four depth charges and an ASW rocket were used for purposes of warning and four more for effective weapons use. A destroyer, torpedo boats, submarines, minesweepers, several other naval vessels, and helicopters all took part in the ASW operations.

• The intruding submarine or submarines eventually leave, undamaged.

One additional important point should be made about the Utö/Huvudskär event. The Defense staff report for 1980 states that during the ASW operations "At one instance in this period observations were made which mean that the submarine's class but not its nationality could be determined."[15] This means that the submarine was identified as a Whisky-class vessel, as these are operated by both the USSR and Poland. A subsequent editorial in the Swedish naval journal specifically referred to it as a "W submarine" (i.e., Whisky-class), and in November 1986, the chief of the Defense staff made this official. A press report in 1981, however, quoted Swedish naval personnel who explictly and repeatedly referred to the vessel as a "Soviet submarine."

The government at this time, as it had been since 1977,

was a coalition of three non-social-democratic parties. Shortly after the March 1980 event the head of the Swedish navy commented that

> The understanding that should exist – and which previously did exist in this country – that one must pay attention to facts and the capabilities of a presumptive attacker, and not to hopes, must return. The understanding that we now have to live with is that the preceding period of détente is over and that the risks are evident that it is the opposite – increasing tension – that we have to live with.[16]

After the October 1980 events, the minister of defense wrote that Sweden's lack of ASW resources was not – or should not be – news: it was the result of a process dating back at least 12 years. He also said that Sweden "must have sufficient resources to carry out its responsibilities in the case that it succeeds in remaining neutral at the time of a crisis in its area." It was also necessary "to raise [Sweden's] capability to deal with a surprise attack, a threat that becomes increasingly significant for [Swedish] defense planning."[17]

1981

A defense policy report by a Swedish parliamentary committee published in February 1981 stated:

> A military defence of such strength and composition as to convince a would-be aggressor that it is not in his interests to utilize Swedish territory, is a precondition for the preservation of respect for Swedish neutrality in the event of war in our immediate vicinity. We must also be capable of intercepting and repulsing violations of Swedish territory and protecting such traffic as we are under an obligation to permit in accordance with the laws of neutrality.
>
> Respect for the integrity of Swedish territory must

be firmly founded and maintained in peacetime by the
ability of our military defence to detect and intercept
violations.

The report added a single sentence regarding submarine
incursions:

> The ability to detect and ward off foreign submarines is
> important: for this reason our existing helicopter units
> should be kept in service and further measures should
> be studied. Protection to shipping should be provided
> by units primarily assigned to other tasks and through
> minelaying.[18]

Submarine violations were virtually continuous in
1981, however:

- January 1981: submarine observed south of Sand-
hammaren, east coast of Skåne.
- February 1981: Navy detects a submarine at Utö
again, in the same area as the September 1980 events.
- March 1981: submarine observed on surface in the
Göteborg archipelago.
- May 1981: warning munitions are used against a sub-
marine near the Havringe lighthouse, Södermanland.
- May 1981: another submarine detected near Gustaf
Dahléns lighthouse in the same area.
- May 13, 1981: submarine detected outside Ronneby
on the east coast of Blekinge, by, among other methods, an
ASW helicopter lowering its dipping sonar directly onto the
submarine with sufficient strength to damage the sonar.[19]
- June 1981: submarine detected near Utö again. Heli-
copter's dipping sonar in this case reportedly gets snagged
in the submarine.
- October 1981: submarine observed outside Sten-
shuvud in Skåne.[20]

In the last week of October 1981, Soviet President
Leonid Brezhnev was due to visit Bonn. In anticipation, the

West German weekly magazine *Der Spiegel* published an interview with Brezhnev on October 26, 1981, which carried the following quotation:

> The road to peace is not through confrontation but . . . through practical steps that help bring peoples closer together, help normalize the international atmosphere and remove such obstacles as mutual distrust, prejudice and fear.[21]

On the very next day, just before 10 p.m. on the evening of October 27, an older Soviet diesel-powered, Whisky-class submarine, number 137, ran aground at Torumskär, 16 nautical miles within one of the two most important Swedish naval base areas in the country, outside Karlskrona in southern Sweden. Attempts made all evening by the submarine to extricate itself failed. In the course of these attempts it had put divers over the side in an attempt to find its way free. The submarine was discovered the next morning by a Swedish fisherman, and when reported to the nearby naval base, Swedish military officers could scarcely believe the report. They arrived on the scene around 11 a.m., more than 12 hours after the stranding took place. The submarine carried no marking or identification. To have reached the place it stranded, it had to navigate in an area of outlying skerries, islands, and grounds, some of which it successfully passed. The submarine had grounded not only far within Swedish internal waters, but also within a restricted security area, and within that, in an area that may have been mined.

Upon being questioned several days later, the Soviet submarine captain claimed that the submarine had been carrying out maneuvers at a depth of 45 meters in the vicinity of Bornholm (Denmark) on the previous days, and that he thought he was some 130 km south of the Swedish coast (just north of the Polish coast) at the time he ran aground.[22] A navigation error of that magnitude, even with a simple compass, is inconceivable. Without navigation aids, and left to random chance, the submarine would have been more likely to run aground on various outlying Swedish islands rather than being able to pass through the narrow channels that it did. The submarine commander also claimed that he had been running on the surface for two hours before grounding. This would, however, have enabled the submarine to be detected by Swedish coastal radars, which were on at the time, and no such detection took place. Visibility was 6 to 11 km at the time the submarine ran aground. If the submarine had been on the surface, it would have easily seen a 31-meter-high unmanned lighthouse that it had passed as well as the land only 150 meters away to either side of it at the terminal stages of its trip. The Swedish naval officers carrying out the interrogation found most of the Soviet explanations preposterous, and if the description of the exchange that appeared in a book published by two Swedish journalists in 1984 reflects what was said, it can best be described as comic theater.[23]

In explaining the failure in navigation to which the submarine commander attributed the grounding, he claimed that all of the following had gone wrong simultaneously:

- the radio navigation equipment was out of order;
- the depth gauge was out of order;
- the gyrocompass had broken down, after a check only an hour before the grounding;
- the magnetic compass and radar on board the submarine had not been used;
- major errors had been made in using the Decca navigation system;
- optical observations had been incorrect. The Soviet captain pointedly noted that they had seen the lighthouse light – it was too difficult to deny, particularly in view of the claim that the submarine had been running on the surface – but that (despite its sweeping pattern) it had been mistaken for a fishing boat's light.

Moreover, when the portions of the Swedish Defense staff report on the grounding that were made public were released on December 18, it was stated that the submarine was most likely to have been in the vicinity of the Swedish coast — perhaps within the restricted security area — since October 24, three days prior to its grounding. It was also determined some time later that the U-137 was taking part in a larger operation of the kind more clearly demonstrated in 1982. The Defense staff report also stated that between October 19 and 23, secret Swedish torpedo tests had been carried out in the vicinity of the Karlskrona base, as well as one on the evening of October 27, of which there had been public notice. Senior Defense spokesmen indicated that Swedish torpedo tests frequently suffer from "surveillance" by uninvited "observers." On October 28, Swedish coastal naval forces were also scheduled to carry out an exercise in closing the Baltic straits.

The first public mention in the USSR of the stranding incident was not made until the event had been entirely resolved and the submarine was on its way home. The official Soviet statement claimed that the submarine was "on an ordinary training cruise in the Baltic" and that virtually all navigation aids had failed simultaneously. The following is the full Soviet communiqué:

> On the night of October 27–28, a Soviet diesel submarine No. 137 on an ordinary training cruise in the Baltic, strayed off course in poor visibility, as a result of the malfunction of navigation instruments and because of resulting errors in determining its location. The submarine ran aground near the South-Eastern extremity of Sweden.
>
> The submarine was refloated by Swedish rescue vessels and after talks with the Swedish authorities, the two sides agreed to consider the incident closed.
>
> The submarine sailed from Swedish territorial waters to her home port.[24]

The submarine was not only within Swedish internal rather than territorial waters, but it was also specifically within one of the two most highly restricted Swedish naval areas, requiring competent navigation to get there, rather than the absence of any. None of this was likely to have been random accident, except for the final grounding.

Faced with a persistent campaign that continued through 1984 and 1985 by several Swedish publicists with access to the major media who argued that the Soviet submarine had indeed grounded by accident, the Swedish Defense staff released further evidence.[25] It was disclosed that the Swedish naval authorities had noted in their investigation on board the submarine that the logbook entries for the gyrocompass course headings in the last 20 minutes of the submarine's voyage had been altered.[26] The submarine's radio navigation device also seemed to be in perfectly adequate operating order. The submarine apparently also contained an inertial navigation system. The heavy diesel engine noise that some local residents reported hearing early in the evening of the stranding was caused by a Swedish torpedo recovery tug and navy helicopters that had been taking part in the torpedo tests and was not the submarine running on the surface. Finally, intercepted radio communications from the Soviet Kashin-class destroyer 446, which was standing by just outside Swedish territorial waters, with Vice Admiral Alexej Kalinin of the Soviet Baltic Fleet on board, ordered the submarine captain to offer the explanation of navigational error.[27]

Two days after the stranding, on October 29, a second submarine was detected 10 km inside Swedish territorial waters in the same general vicinity of the approaches to Karlskrona. Elements of the Soviet Baltic Fleet also gathered just outside the territorial border line: by October 28, two destroyers, a submarine salvage vessel, a geodetic ship, two tugboats, and two Elint vessels; and by November 4, an additional destroyer, two missile corvettes, a frigate, and an oiler. The USSR apparently at first expected that the submarine would simply be released by Sweden as the USSR requested. Soviet authorities had also asked to be able to remove the submarine from its ground themselves and for their embassy personnel in Stockholm to have access to the submarine. When Sweden denied these requests and indicated that it had procedures of its own in mind, the Soviet Foreign Ministry protested strongly to the Swedish ambassador in Moscow. The Swedish government put four demands to the USSR. These were

- that the USSR apologize for the intrusion,
- that the USSR pay for the salvage costs,
- that the submarine be salvaged by Swedish vessels,
- that the submarine commander and other of its officers be questioned—on a Swedish vessel or on Swedish soil.[28]

The USSR accepted the first three conditions, but resisted the fourth until November 2, by which time the submarine had been grounded for six days. The Soviet officers were questioned outside the security zone, and Swedish officers were permitted to examine the navigation equipment and the logbook on board the submarine. It developed that a senior Soviet naval officer, a submarine squadron commander in the Baltic fleet, Commander Josef Avsukjevitj, was also on board the submarine. A Soviet deputy foreign minister—with 10 Soviet admirals lined up silently behind him—called in the Swedish ambassador in Moscow and demanded that Sweden release the submarine. Sweden was blowing up a small incident in a way that could harm Soviet-Swedish relations. Sweden had overstepped the boundaries of good neighborly relations by the manner in which it was interrogating the Soviet officers. Sweden would be responsible for the consequences if such behavior were repeated. The Soviet ambassador in Stockholm also complained that the Soviet officers were being treated in a scandalous manner by being questioned. When Swedish officers expressed their amazement at the nature of some of the replies during the questioning, the Soviet officers reportedly protested that the remarks contravened proper naval behavior. On another occasion they also objected to photographs being taken of the submarine as a violation of their integrity.[29]

Among the other extraordinary aspects of the grounding of the U-137, perhaps the most surprising of all was the announcement that the Swedish government believed that the submarine carried nuclear weapons. Swedish Prime Minister Thorbjörn Fälldin announced at a press conference on November 5, the evening before the Soviet submarine was to leave Swedish waters, that the government believed the submarine "is in all probability armed with nuclear warheads."[30] As the submarine lay aground, its bow section was somewhat elevated and the Swedish Defense Research Institute (FOA), an agency of the Swedish Ministry of Defense, began a series of radiation measurements from outside the hull. These were begun from a small boat on the evening of October 29 and then continued for two more days with more sophisticated equipment from inside the hull of a Swedish coast guard vessel that was tethered alongside the bow of the submarine. Using gamma ray spectroscopy, it was determined that about 10 kg (22 pounds) of Uranium 238 (U-238) was detectable just inside the torpedo tube section.[31]

The Swedish government then

> informed the Soviet Government that in all probability nuclear weapons were present on board the submarine. In order to be able to establish the presence of nuclear warheads with absolute certainty, further measurements and investigations of the torpedoes themselves were necessary. In view of this, we made a pressing request to the Soviet Government that Swedish experts should be given access to the submarine so that they could establish whether there were nuclear weapons on board.[32]

The USSR's reply was significant in that it did not deny that there were nuclear weapons on board:

The Soviet submarine 137 carries, as do all other naval vessels at sea, the necessary weapons and ammunition. However, this has nothing to do with the circumstances surrounding the unintentional intrusion by the submarine into Sweden's territorial waters.[33]

The Swedish government pointedly noted, both to the Soviet ambassador in Stockholm and in public,

The Soviet reply means, as far as we can see, that Moscow does not deny the presence of nuclear weapons on board. It also implies, although it does not actually say so, that the Soviet Government refuses to allow Swedish experts to carry out an inspection.[34]

The second point of the Swedish assessment appears gratuitous, but no inspection of the torpedoes was attempted. Swedish Foreign Minister Ola Ullsten also noted that "it is also most remarkable that a submarine which is in such a deficient technical state is at the same time equipped with nuclear weapons."

The Swedish protest note stated:

The investigation made by the supreme commander shows that there is no question of faulty navigation being the main reason for the intrusion into Swedish territory. On the basis of the investigation the Swedish Government draws the conclusion that the Soviet submarine intentionally violated Swedish territory for the purpose of carrying on illegal activities. The Swedish Government is compelled to note with dismay and indignation that the grounded submarine in the Karlskrona Archipelago probably has one or more nuclear warheads on board. . . .

On account of the extreme importance of the matter, the Swedish Government has immediately demanded that the Soviet Government present a clarification as to whether or not nuclear weapons are present on board the submarine. The Soviet Government has ignored the request of the Swedish Government for clarification on this point. The Swedish Government must interpret this as implying that the Soviet Government has been unable to deny the presence of nuclear weapons on board the submarine.

The Swedish Government must make a sharp protest to the Government of the Soviet Union against the violation of Swedish territory and of a Swedish military prohibited area intentionally committed by the Soviet submarine 137.

The Swedish Government finds this flagrant violation of Swedish territory all the more remarkable and serious since in all probability the submarine has carried nuclear weapons into Swedish territory. The Swedish Government demands that the Soviet Union prevent any repetition of this flagrant violation of Sweden's territorial integrity and of the fundamental principles of international law.[35]

In his public remarks, Prime Minister Fälldin added that,

Finally, we demand in our note of protest to the Soviet Government that it prevent any repetition of these violations of Swedish territorial integrity and of the fundamental principles of international law.

The prime minister also noted that it was "the most remarkable and serious violation of Sweden's territorial integrity since the second World War."

The submarine was released the next day. Upon its release, the USSR rejected the Swedish protest note, complaining that the Swedish government statement was "devoid of any legal and factual grounds," that it had not displayed a "correct attitude" or made an "objective appraisal," and had violated

the generally recognised principle of international law under which a warship enjoys complete immunity from the jurisdiction of any state other than the one under whose flag she is sailing.

Even if a foreign warship fails to observe a coastal

state's rules on passage through its territorial waters, the only thing the coastal state may do is demand that she leave its waters. . . .

At the end of the Swedish statement, the demand is made that "a repetition of this gross violation be prevented." In this particular case it sounds like a demand that the very possibility of accidents occurring at sea be excluded. This demand is simply not compatible with common sense.

The Government of the Soviet Union firmly rejects the protest contained in the statement by the Swedish Government as being groundless in both law and fact.

The Soviet Government has always sincerely strived, and continues to strive, to develop all-round relations with Sweden in the spirit of mutual respect, good-neighbourliness and co-operation.

It would like to hope that the Government of Sweden, for its part, will adhere to the same course in relations between the two neighbouring countries.[36]

Perhaps the most remarkable portion of the Soviet reply was the gratuitous and purposeful insistence that a repetition of gross violations — transmuted into "the very possibility of accidents at sea" — could *not* be prevented. Such a demand "is simply not compatible with common sense." Given the particular occasion of the statement and the generally oblique language of diplomatic notes on crucial points, it seems clear that the Soviet Union was providing advance notice that whatever the nature of the submarine program it had no intention of stopping it.

On the same day that the USSR published its rejection note, the Soviet news agency Tass also released a story claiming that Sweden was spying on the USSR, and the Soviet embassy in Washington gave 10 selected journalists a forged "secret agreement" between the United States and Sweden under which the United States allegedly had access to the Swedish naval base at Karlskrona.[37] The Soviet rejection note did not once mention nuclear weapons. The accompanying Tass dispatch, however, claimed that it was

"NATO specialists" who had alleged the detection of the U-238, that all of the allegations were "inventions . . . evidently intended for ignoramuses." The Tass report added that the U.S. Central Intelligence Agency (CIA) spread the rumors because it wanted to harm détente and that the NATO experts alleged the detection of radiation to discredit the idea of a Nordic Nuclear-Free Zone and to facilitate the deployment of new U.S. missiles in Europe. Another Soviet official interviewed in Oslo claimed that the radiation the Swedes measured must have come from their wristwatches.[38]

Some weeks later, Soviet officials interviewed by Sweden's major daily newspaper blamed the entire affair on

> Swedish forces that want to undermine the relations between the USSR and Sweden. But the Soviet side is open for a dialogue. We are not closing any doors for a renewed development of relations between our two countries. But it cannot be one-sided: both sides are necessary in order to develop relationships.[39]

Some weeks after the stranding of the Soviet submarine, Foreign Minister Ullsten again explained that the 1972 defense decision was responsible for the fact that Sweden had few ships suitable for ASW. Those were clearly not the capabilities that were missing in this case, however. Rather, there seemed to be no functioning sensor systems in peacetime. Nevertheless, government actions to increase either ship or sensor capabilities were few during the two electoral mandate periods during which nonsocialist governments held office, from 1976 to 1982. The appropriation for two new ships to replace the demobilized destroyers was obtained. The government's 1982 defense decision involved a slight increase in military expenditure based on a revision of a complicated compensation formula for wage and price increases. Defense expenditure as a percent of gross national product (GNP) dropped, however, from 3.1 to 2.8 percent from 1976 to 1982. Despite this, the Social Democratic Party congress in 1981 decided to seek direct reductions in total defense expenditure, including civil defense and economic defense stockpiling, and particularly in the military expenditure allocation — reportedly for the first time since the end of World War II. When the Social Democrats returned to office in October 1982, they did reduce military expenditure by approximately $50 million, a reduction of about 1.5 percent, with the approval of one of the nonsocialist parties and no strong opposition from the others, despite the major 1982 events that had by then intervened.

After the stranding of the U-137, Swedish naval sources commented that foreign submarine incursions "appeared to be the rule rather than the exception" and offered the first suggestions as to possible motives:

- The Defense staff felt certain that the U-137 had, among other missions, been observing the Swedish torpedo tests.
- Following the major events that took place at the end of 1982, it was noticed that Swedish mine chains had been tampered with in several locations, presumably by foreign divers. The submarine's objective might also therefore have been to inspect the disposition of mine chains in the area of Karlskrona.[40]
- More general suggestions were "activities of an intelligence character, and direct preparations for an eventual attack against Sweden . . . [or] preparations to utilize Swedish territory in a war in which Sweden was neutral . . . [or] possibilities of utilizing Swedish territorial waters as launching areas for [submarine-launched] nuclear missiles."[41]

1982

The events that took place in 1982 constitute a connected series of four important parts that continued into 1983:

1. The events themselves, particularly the publicly reported major events, in October 1982;

2. The report on the events, prepared by a Swedish government commission and released in April 1983;

3. The Swedish government's public protest and notes to the USSR and the government's private messages for the same purpose, April 1983;

4. The Soviet response: the events in Sundsvall, Töre, etc., in May 1983.

The Soviet response to the outcome of the U-137, October 1981 stranding was both prompt and definitive: The number of detected submarine intrusions jumped to between 40 and 50 in 1982, from an annual average of around 10 in the previous half dozen years. There were four major "operations"—as they came to be categorized in official Swedish terminology—of intruding submarines during the year. Only one of these, which took place in the fall of 1982, received major public attention, however. The location and nature of the others, as well as whether there were any Swedish military or government responses to them, received only brief mention in the public press, or none at all. One of the larger operations was apparently at Kvarken in June 1982 and a second at Landsort in August 1982. The government was nonsocialist until October 1982. The submarines were noted as follows:[42]

• June 1982: submarine observed near Sandhamn, in the Stockholm archipelago;

• June 1982: submarine detected in the north Kvarken area. ASW over several days produced repeated definite contacts;

• June 1982: helicopter detects submarine near Väddö in the Stockholm archipelago and uses depth charges;

• July 1982: submarine observed north of Väddö;

• August 1982: repeated submarine contacts near Landsort in the Stockholm archipelago, major Swedish ASW operations.

The description that follows of the events in September and October 1982 is based upon Swedish government sources that only became available in April and June 1983. The information was for the most part not available at the time of the events themselves, and important portions of it were not included in the subsequent report of the government commission.[43] The activities began in the last week in September. They coincided with a change in the government administration as a result of recent elections. For the first eight days of the operations, the incumbent nonsocialist administration was still in office, after which the incoming Social Democratic administration under Prime Minister Olof Palme took office. Active Swedish ASW operations lasted until around October 20, and the operations were discontinued on November 1. Two submarines and two midget submarines had been operating in the area of Hårsfjärden, deep inside Swedish internal waters and in immediate proximity to Sweden's major naval base, Muskö. It was assumed that one submarine served as the mother vessel for each midget submarine. A midget submarine entered Stockholm harbor proper in the last week of September in what is presumed to be a part of the same operation. In addition, a submarine entered Oxelösund harbor on October 2.

Identification of the intruding submarine's nationality was made on the basis of optical observations of submarine mast configurations, by acoustical and Elint recordings, and by examination of the keel impression left by a submarine resting on the mud bottom outside of Hårsfjärden near Mälsten. All these identifications independently implicated Warsaw Pact submarines, in most cases Whisky-class submarines. Acoustic recordings indicated two propellers and in addition provided a frequency analysis of the engine sounds, which more closely identify the submarine.[44] A measurement of the width of the keel impression left in the mud bottom by one of the submarines reportedly matched within centimeters the width of the keel of the U-137, which the Swedish Defense Ministry had measured while it was stranded in Gåsfjärden in October 1981. Whisky-class sub-marines have a reinforced keel as well as a double propeller. Communications intercepts also identified Warsaw Pact submarines. Finally Elint recordings, which were made of emitting submarine radars, can in some cases determine not only vessel class, but also the individual vessel. At the time of the events, the USSR operated 45 conventionally powered submarines in the Baltic, of which the majority were Whisky-class vessels, while Poland had only four oper-ational Whisky-class submarines.

The midget submarines were apparently of two differ-ent types, one of which was a double-tracked vehicle capa-ble of crawling on the sea floor as well as moving by conven-tional submarine propeller propulsion. The report issued by the SDC contained photographs of the tracks left by the vehicle. As early in 1973, *Pravda* published a photograph of a Soviet double-tracked underwater vehicle that had been operating in the waters near the Azores — according to Sovi-et sources, searching for "the lost continent of Atlantis" — in a region with substantial U.S. subsurface ASW equipment. The USSR has been developing underwater vehicles since the mid-1960s and has additionally purchased some from Western suppliers, such as Canadian manufacturers. In 1985 the British military *Recognition Journal* published illustrations of 12 different Soviet submersibles, some of which may have civilian uses, with the clear implication that there may be additional military submersibles not in-cluded in the illustrations.[45]

There is some possibility that in 1983 and 1984 the USSR used a third kind of midget submarine in addition to the two that were used in the October 1982 operations, and the Swedish military claims to have a "definite understand-ing" of the midget submarines that have operated in inter-nal Swedish waters, which they have not made public.[46] Bot-tom tracks produced by submersibles were found in additional areas in 1983 to 1985 where they had not been before. It also now seemed likely that the submarines detected and chased by the Swedish navy in 1980 and 1981 were "mother submarines," forced to await the return of their midget submarines from deeper penetration missions. This served to explain their tactic of not leaving Swedish internal and territorial waters when detected and warned, but remaining and going even deeper into the archipelago. The behavior of the submarines could now be explained, not as deliberately "provocative" or flaunting, but determined by the function they were performing: they could not leave until they had recovered their midget submarines. At times they exposed themselves as diversionary tactics to enable a recovery to take place in another nearby area. (In 1985 the Soviet naval journal *Morskoi Sbornik* [Naval Anthology] rather surprisingly published two articles entitled "Expenditure for Diversionary Attack Forces Against Ships in Bases" and "Trends in Development Abroad of Small Underwater Attack Submersibles."[47])

On July 17, 1982, as a consequence of the 1981 events — the Swedish government had published a new IKFN ordinance, which replaced the one of January 1967. As published it was not to go into operation until July 1, 1983. The government quickly gave permission for its application, however, as the October events began.

> The defence authorities for the first time applied principles which meant that a submarine entering internal waters should be forced to the surface. The purpose of the anti-submarine operation, and of the use of armed force, was thus to force the intruders to the surface for identification and further measures. . . . these rules of engagement for anti-submarine operations had not previously been applied. . . .[48]

The new regulation stated that

> a foreign submarine which is found to be submerged within Swedish internal waters shall be forced to the surface. It shall then be commanded to heave to, be

identified, and then taken to an anchorage for further action. If necessary, force of arms may be resorted to.

A foreign submarine which is found to be submerged within the territorial sea shall be turned away from the territory. If necessary, force of arms may be resorted to.

Should special circumstances so require, the Supreme Commander may order recourse to force of arms without prior warning against a foreign submarine which is found to be submerged within Swedish territory.[49]

Previously the submarine, no matter where it was located, was only to be turned away. Even in the new regulation the distinction regarding location was crucial.

In the first place, an important distinction is made between Swedish internal waters, i.e., all waters inside the so-called "base lines" (the lines connecting the outermost rocks and skerries), on the one hand, and, on the other, Sweden's territorial sea, the area between these base lines and the territorial limits which Sweden extended on 1 July, 1979, from 4 to 12 nautical miles.

There is a difference between these parts of Swedish territory in international law, in that inner waters are equated with Swedish land territory in the sense that as a coastal state Sweden there enjoys unrestricted sovereignty, while in the territorial sea the warships of a foreign power are entitled to "innocent passage" in accordance with certain specific rules (including prior notification, and a requirement that any submarines pass through on the surface and flying their national ensign).[50]

The severity of application of the IKFN regulations evolved with time, and there remained variation in the actual operational practices during individual events. At first one depth charge was used, off target. Then four, still off target. Finally four more were used, allegedly more or less on target. Specific permission of the commander in chief was still required to detonate mines, and in actual practice this meant that the decision was deferred to the prime minister. This remained the case in the spring of 1984, when both the prime minister and the defense minister were out of the country during important portions of a month-long ASW operation. It is also clear that there were definite cases in which orders were given to withhold the use of munitions in the case of mines, and such instances are explicitly discussed in the SDC report. Forty-seven depth charges and five mines were used in the Hårsfjärden ASW operations, spanning a period of nearly a month. Swedish authorities have never again raised the question of whether the Soviet submarines in this or any of the other incidents subsequent to the October 1981 U-137 stranding might also be armed with nuclear weapons.

As early as October 21, 1982, the Swedish government decided to establish an investigative commission, the SDC, and it was to report its findings in April 1983. The commission's chairman had been defense minister in an earlier Social Democratic government, and the commission's report was made public. The commission found that

> Hårsfjärden is the most serious violation of Swedish territory to date that has given rise to a Swedish anti-submarine operation.
>
> This operation was thus the largest effort employed in any incident by Swedish defence forces during the post-war period, both as regards time-scale and personnel, and the scale of the material resources used. . . .
>
> Swedish territory is now being violated by conventional submarines carrying minisubmarines, which are then released to penetrate deep into our archipelagos. . . .
>
> But the most essential aspect was and continues to be the general observation that submarine violations of Swedish territory have shown a tendency in recent years to increase. It has been possible in particular to note that the intruder submarines have begun to be-

have in a more openly provocative manner, partly by refusing to allow themselves to be turned back, instead undertaking diversionary and evasive manoeuvres in response to attempts on the part of the Swedish Navy to turn them away.[51]

The commission also found "that the violations at Hårsfjärden, *and other violations during 1980–1982, were by submarines belonging to the Warsaw Pact.*[52] (Author's emphasis.)

    This finding implicated the USSR in a rather large number of incidents in addition to Hårsfjärden and the U-137 stranding. The Swedish government's protest note, following the publication of the commission's report, was made directly to the Soviet Union and not to Poland or "the Warsaw Pact." The commission not only evaluated the Hårsfjärden incident, but also looked into the other reported incursions during 1982 and found a pattern that included at least four "waves" of submarines entering different parts of Swedish territorial waters at evidently coordinated times.

> The commission also concluded that the submarine incursions continued in late 1982 and early 1983. A month after the dramatic intrusion into Hårsfjärden, a new intrusion by the same kind of midget submarine was confirmed in the same general area. Other observations led to the conclusion that there had been at least two additional intrusions into (the) Stockholm archipelago, as well as at least three violations of Swedish territorial waters in the vicinity of the Karlskrona base area in southern Sweden. A series of indications in the southern part of Stockholm Archipelago in mid-April would seem to suggest that another major operation was undertaken at that time.[53]

The November 1982 events — barely a month after Hårsfjärden — took place in the nearby north Mysingen area, and new bottom crawler tracks were found of the same type that had been found inside Hårsfjärden.[54] Karlskrona was the area in which the U-137 had stranded in 1981 and in which the major events of 1984 would take place. The midget submarines operated repeatedly in the same areas, near the two major Swedish naval bases and major civilian port facilities and often used the same channels for their operations.

The submarine commission's report described — as did numerous other Swedish statements, before and after, particularly from military sources — the difficulties of sonar detection in the irregular, shallow archipelago, with varying salinity and fresh water combinations and echoes caused by irregular bottom contours. These are conditions that admittedly provide complicating problems for ASW detection sensors that are not faced in the same degree of severity in the open ocean areas of more uniform water temperature and salinity. The Norwegian government report on the Hardangerfjord events similarly described the difficulties of sonar operation in very deep bays. In the Swedish case, however, it is difficult to avoid the conclusion that a major part of the problem was the nearly total lack of appropriate equipment rather than deficits in its optimal functioning.

At the time of the Hårsfjärden events, Sweden's ASW capabilities appear to have been as follows:[55]

• The destroyer *Halland*, apparently the last ship fitted with a variable depth sonar, entered Muskö naval base for ceremonies ending its active service on the very day that the Hårsfjärden events began. Despite the equipment that it carried, its previous experience in ASW operations, and its immediate availability in the area, it remained tied up at dockside and was not used in the ASW operations for administrative reasons.

• Two new coastal corvettes were being built at the time for delivery to the navy in 1985–1986 and four more were subsequently ordered, the first of which could be delivered by 1989. All of these were to be equipped with variable depth sonars.

Some Basic Elements of Submarine Detection

In using active sonar, a searching vessel or helicopter-suspended device emits sound waves that produce an echo on striking a submarine. A series of such echoes provides the submarine's course, speed, and depth, as well as its bearing from the transmitter. Range is, however, limited, and the hunted submarine will detect the searching sound and can use tactical or electronic countermeasures, as well as active decoys. A submarine moving in a radial direction from the sound transmitter (that is, in an arc) produces a shift in the frequency of the echoes. This frequency shift, known as the doppler effect, is not produced by a stationary object, echoes from bottom surface contours, or a submarine with its axis in line with the transmitter. This is one of the reasons that it is always desirable to have two ASW helicopters operating close together. A helicopter's active sonor can nevertheless detect a stationary submarine by frequency modulation of its emitted sound signal. This capability is again increased by using two helicopters simultaneously.

Another class of active sonar is high frequency, or side-scan, sonars. They have a shorter range, but are less affected by varying water conditions such as exist in the Baltic archipelagos. They are specifically designed to detect immobile objects on the sea floor and would therefore detect a stationary submarine. A stationary submarine can be clearly detected at a range of 2 to 3 km by the kind of high frequency sonar carried by civilian maritime hazard survey ships. West Germany, for example, operates such a civilian survey vessel in the Baltic. In addition to their military versions, side-scan sonars are commercially available and have been routinely used by marine archaeologists since the late 1960s.

Passive sonar, basically a hydrophone (a device in the water that can detect sound), has a much longer range and does not disclose the presence of the hunting ship. It is more difficult, however, to obtain an accurate indication of the submarine's range, depth, and bearing using a passive sonar. Passive sonars can also be mounted on the sea floor in chains connected to ground stations or mounted on buoys that can telemeter their data to ships or aircraft. They are also used for recording submarine or other ship engine sound signatures. Finally, if a submarine uses its own active sonars, standard intercept equipment can provide measurement of the bearing, pulse length, and frequency of the hostile sonars. This provides information that can also be used to identify the submarine's nationality, in addition to its immediate tactical use.

In summary, methods of detecting submarines based on sound detection in water are divided into active and passive sonar. The specific devices can exist in many forms: attached to ship or submarine hulls, towed behind ships (variable depth sonar, and arrays), lowered into the water from a helicopter (dipping sonar), fixed to the sea floor or bays, or attached to buoys and suspended in the water to any depth desired. Nonacoustic methods are also used, of which there are primarily three: magnetic anomaly detectors (MAD) – making use of the submarine's metallic construction – infrared, and laser detectors for penetration of relatively shallow waters (of approximately 30 meters).

The following references provide the interested reader with some basic sources on the functioning of sonar and other ASW systems:

- Robert A. Frosch, "Underwater Sound," *International Science and Technology* 1, no. 9 (September 1962): 40–46.
- G. R. Lindsey, "The Submarine Environment," *Survival* 6, no. 2 (March–April 1964): 69–76.
- Ralph Hightower, "Underwater Weapons and Ordnance" in F. B. Pollard and J. H. Arnold Jr., *Aerospace Ordnance Handbook* (Prentice Hall: Englewood, N.J., 1966), 395–421.
- "Undersea Weapon Systems: Special Report," *Space/Aeronautics* 33, no. 1 (January 1960): 21–109.
- Frank Leary, "Search for Subs," *Space/Aeronautics* 44, no. 4 (September 1965): 58–68.

- Capt. Thomas B. McGrath, *A Perspective on Antisubmarine Warfare*, R-19 (Washington, D.C.: Data Publications, [undated]), 132 pages.
- Capt. Robert H. Smith, "ASW – The Crucial Challenge," *United States Naval Institute Proceedings* 98, no. 5 (May 1972): 127-141.
- Richard L. Garwin, "Antisubmarine Warfare and National Security," *Scientific American* 227, no. 1 (July 1972): 14-25.
- and in Swedish, *Marin Nytt* (Navy News), no. 6 (1981): 7-15, and "ASW With Helicopters" *Marin Nytt*, no. 6 (1980): 5-9.

A compendium of military ASW systems in standard use in the mid-1970s is available in The Stockholm International Peace Research Institute (SIPRI), *Tactical and Strategic Antisubmarine Warfare* (Cambridge, Mass.: The MIT Press, 1974), 53-148.

- The first of a new class of six minesweepers was also to be delivered to the navy in 1984. These were all to be equipped with a high frequency mine-searching sonar, which was not previously carried by Swedish minesweepers and which can effectively detect stationary submarines at a range of 1.5 km. The only Swedish ship equipped with a side-scan sonar was the hydrographic vessel, *Belos*, which reportedly used the sonar to find the bottom tracks after the Hårsfjärden events. At times during the Hårsfjärden ASW operations, the submarines were reported as stationary, which would have optimized the use of the side-scan sonar. Side-scan sonar was commercially available, however, and could have been quickly fitted to virtually every Swedish ship afloat – in fact, to any outboard vessel 20-25 feet in length.
- There were no sonar arrays or signal processing facilities, and centralized peacetime naval command centers did

not seem to have any direct input from submarine detection sensors.

• Swedish capability for frequency analysis is sometimes described as having existed since the 1970s and so excellent that an individual ship motor signature can be compared to computer-stored records to determine class, ship, and number. At other times, as in 1986, it is described as so abysmally poor as to make it impossible to distinguish Soviet from Danish twin-screwed submarines.

• The FOA had reportedly tested a helicopter-mounted laser bathometer (depth gauge) for submarine detection in relatively shallow waters since 1981. There is no record of its performance in actual ASW operations.

• The entire burden of ASW detection and tracking for all of Sweden rested on seven helicopters. Their ASW mission had been anticipated to be convoy escort to Gotland, and their sonar performed most satisfactorily against a moving target in the open sea.

• Bottom-mounted MAD, which register the passing of a submarine, existed. These should be particularly effective in narrow, shallow passages, compensating for problems with inshore sonar. How many were manned in peacetime is unclear. There is no public knowledge of the degree to which they may be prone to producing spurious signals. Detection sensors fitted to mine systems were also allegedly optimized for surface ships rather than submarines.

• There was no airborne MAD. In 1981, the Swedish Coast Guard contributed a single twin-engined Cessna aircraft with an infrared detection pod that could be used in reconnaissance for snorkeling submarines. It was used on an experimental basis, particularly from July to December 1983. Then, after further trials, it was decided late in 1985 to purchase two more for the Coast Guard (primarily to search for oil spills) as well as a used aircraft for the navy.

• It is not clear at what point the Swedish navy first understood that it was chasing midget submarines – apparently during the Hårsfjärden event, if not before. In 1984, the navy purchased a small Yugoslav underwater vehicle to use in testing and found it extremely difficult to detect.

In conclusion, gross deficits in Swedish ASW capabilities were manifest. Nevertheless, as Carl Bildt, the Swedish Moderate Party's defense specialist, has pointed out,

> the Norwegian Navy with its frigates, German-built submarines, U.S.-supplied P-3 Orions and access to Sosus data has so far not been more successful than its self-reliant, neutral Swedish counterpart in handling this new and very complicated threat.[56]

It is here that the other half of the puzzle — the intentions of the ASW operation and the effect of operational orders on performance — enters the picture. Norwegian statements that sinking a submarine was avoided have been noted. During the Hårsfjärden events, Sweden used mines as an antisubmarine weapon for the first time in peacetime, and the submarine commission's report noted that the use of mines in particular "pose[d] in acute form the balancing act between efforts to force intruder submarines to the surface and the risk of unintentional sinking." The commission's report explicitly stated that mines were not detonated directly on indication of a submarine passing over MAD chains even when the indications were directly observed by service personnel.

> The purpose of detonating the mines, however, as in the case of other weapons use, was to force up passing submarines to the surface, so that those responsible deliberately refrained from automatically detonating mines, and attempted instead a flexible, more sophisticated technique of delayed detonation after indication.[57]

Given the combination of the submarine's speed and the requirement that a charge explode within 5 to 10 meters from a submarine in order to produce serious damage, only

12 to 15 seconds delay allows the submarine to pass out of range of damage. The "flexible, more sophisticated technique" provided that delay. In May 1983, at the time of the Sundsvall ASW operations, it was reported that in the previous fall, during the Hårsfjärden events, mine station chiefs were ordered "to wait some seconds in order to give the submarine a better chance to clear itself." Nevertheless, orders were reportedly still being given in May 1983 to withhold mine detonation on direct indication of a target.[58]

The commission felt compelled to deny charges that the intruding submarines were let go, but was nevertheless forced to explain that the effective result was the escape of the submarines. The commission noted that there were "certain bans on the use of fire in force during the Hårsfjärden operation."

> The Commission has found that the idea that Sweden deliberately let the submarine go stems in general from the question of the "order to withhold fire," i.e., speculation that the submarine escaped in conjunction with or as a consequence of the order to withhold fire issued from time to time by the Defence Command. In addition to speculation that an order to withhold fire, relative primarily to the mines, was issued for the express purpose of permitting submarines to slip out, suggestions have been made that submarines were given an opportunity to get away in conjunction with orders to withhold fire, which admittedly were not issued to this end, but nonetheless had this effect.[59]

The commission also made a point that caution was still a prime consideration and that restraint had been observed:

> the restraint that was natural and necessary, taking into account the fact that the incident, in spite of all, took place in peacetime. . . . and observing also the limitation of armed force consequent upon the objective of forcing the intruder submarine up the surface . . . .the Central Defence Command interven[ed] directly in the operational command, in order to assure that live weap-

ons were used with a restrictiveness corresponding to the objective in hand, and with a satisfactory degree of safety.[60]

It is not clear if this caution differed at all during the portions of the operation that took place under the nonsocialist and socialist governments. The important question for the years to come was whether the policy changed.

The commission's report also did not shy away from making explicit the great degree of confusion that developed in the chain of command during the operations. It did, however, reject the rumors, resulting from the operations' failure, alleging that the submarines were deliberately allowed to escape.[61]

1983

The report of the SDC was released on April 26, 1983. The Swedish government simultaneously delivered a strong protest note to the USSR along with a copy of the report. Prime Minister Palme made an additional public statement and various remarks at press conferences. The Swedish ambassador in Moscow was called home. The note to the USSR stated:

> It is apparent from the report that after a very careful study of all the available information, the Commission has made the judgement that Soviet submarines have violated Swedish territory both in Hårsfjärden Bay and in certain other areas.
>
> The Swedish Government has no information that contradicts the Commission's conclusion in this respect. It concludes that the submarines involved were Soviet submarines.
>
> On this account, the Swedish Government conveys to the Government of the Soviet Union a strong protest against the gross violations of Swedish territorial integrity of which the Soviet navy has been guilty. These violations constitute a grave breach of the rules of in-

ternational law, the upholding of which is an obligation and a common interest of all states. The violations must be interpreted as elements in deliberate and unlawful attempts to explore Sweden's sea territory. This activity must be strongly condemned.

The Swedish Government requests the Government of the Soviet Union to give such instructions to the Soviet navy that the violations of Swedish territory cease.[62]

Palme also said,

It is our responsibility and our determined intention with all the resources we have at our disposal to maintain Sweden's territorial integrity. . . . [the sharpened IKFN regulations] . . . are to clarify that Sweden is prepared in every way to prevent a repetition of the violations that have taken place against our territory.[63]

The prime minister used the phrase "with all the means at our disposal" on several occasions in regard to the manner in which future ASW operations would be carried out, while simultaneously pointing out that "we have previously demonstrated a degree of leniency in our reactions. But this is the last straw. Whoever plans to violate Swedish territory will have to consider that Sweden will now sink submarines."[64] His remarks to an English-language interviewer were even stronger:

"We represent a united nation in our sharp protest," he said at a news conference. "It is crucial to the credibility of our neutrality to show that we can defend our own territory. Violators in the future can count on the Swedish government to order the military to sink the intruder at once."

Later, in a brief interview, he said the Swedish navy's rules of engagement had been changed to permit senior commanders to open fire at once on vessels violating territorial waters. Orders to sink the vessels would come promptly from Stockholm, he promised, if

the vessels remained. . . . What is critical is "that they
stop these grave breaches of international law so that
we don't have to waste time chasing their submarines
around the archipelago."[65]

In televised interviews with the Swedish press, Palme
was much more careful on that point, refusing to commit
himself as to whether orders to sink a submarine would be
given and repeating only that such an eventuality might
take place if the submarine intrusions persisted. He repeatedly emphasized "the risk" that it was impossible to rule out
a sinking occurring unintentionally during the ASW operations and that the intruding submarines constantly ran
that risk. The new IKFN regulations themselves definitely
did not provide orders "to sink" a submarine. It is clear that
that was explicitly avoided during the Hårsfjärden events,
and the emphasis in all the subsequent events remained on
"forcing the submarine to the surface."

Prime Minister Palme also initiated a private back
channel with Soviet officials, which was, however, not publicly disclosed until December 1983, and then only partially
and very much against the government's wishes, in circumstances that rapidly blossomed into a full-blown domestic
political scandal known as the Ferm affair. Full disclosure
of the back channel did not take place until May 1984. On
April 27, the day following the release of the submarine
commission's report in Stockholm, the Swedish ambassador to the United Nations, Anders Ferm, acting as a personal messenger of the prime minister, met in New York
City with Michael Milstein, on May 2 with Georgi Arbatov,
and on May 3 with Milstein again. Milstein was a retired
Soviet lieutenant general who had been a senior officer in
the Soviet military's Chief Intelligence Directorate (GRU),
and Arbatov was director of the U.S.A. and Canada Institute of the USSR's Academy of Sciences, but more essentially a Soviet government emissary. Both men had been
involved for the previous three years with the independent
Commission on Security and Disarmament Issues—known

as the "Palme Commission" – of which Ferm had been the executive secretary. The topic of their discussions were the Soviet submarine violations. Ferm had a simple message that the Swedish government wanted transmitted to Moscow:

> The Swedish government was concerned that its message as to how seriously it viewed the violations was not reaching those who had political responsibility. We want to be certain that some sufficiently senior political leader receives our protest, and takes a decision that the violations should cease, and sees to it that the decision is carried out. *Sweden wants to have a signal that such a decision has been taken. . . .* Sweden wants to have binding assurances in some form from the USSR that they
> 1) respect Sweden's borders
> 2) respect Sweden's neutrality
> 3) will not consciously send submarines into Swedish waters. (Author's emphasis)[66]

Palme personally transmitted the same three points on May 5 to the Soviet ambassador in Stockholm, Boris Pankin.[67] Both Milstein and Arbatov promised to deliver the message when they returned to Moscow within a day or two, and Milstein reportedly stated that "This will have an effect in Moscow, perhaps not immediately, but it will have an effect." Milstein also "made it clear that the USSR would not admit to any territorial violations even if the evidence was indisputable." In subsequent months, Palme met with Arbatov in the Hague on June 18–19, and Swedish Defense Minister Anders Thunborg also met Arbatov in Switzerland around June 23. There is no public information regarding the nature of these other meetings. Thunborg, without giving details, has claimed in a public interview that he told the Soviets with whom he was speaking that the USSR should acknowledge its activities.[68]

On April 25, 1983, the day before the submarine commission report was made public and only a few days before his May 2 meeting with Ambassador Ferm, Arbatov was in Washington as the speaker at one of the Carnegie Endowment's Face to Face seminars. In a rather stormy session that dealt primarily with European security issues, Arbatov was asked a question about the Soviet submarine intrusions into Swedish internal waters. Without admitting Soviet responsibility or actually predicting the continuation of the intrusions, Arbatov remarked that he did not know exactly what had happened, that it could have been any country's submarine, that we all know that submarines operate in other people's waters, and therefore he didn't understand what all the fuss was about. The countries concerned had to accept that such activity would take place.[69]

The Swedish embassy in Washington corroborated Arbatov's remarks in three successive cables (May 11, May 13, and May 17) after questioning a sizable number of the seminar's participants. Nevertheless, the press spokesman of the Swedish Ministry of Foreign Affairs stated that the ministry's understanding was that the press accounts were inaccurate (which they were not in their essential point), and Prime Minister Palme said that "We must base Swedish neutrality policy on concrete events and official statements and not on more or less unsubstantiated rumors from luncheons in Washington."[70] Arbatov himself described the reports as "a premediated provocation with the purpose of damaging the relations between the USSR and Sweden."[71] What no one seems to have noticed was that Arbatov's essential message was no more than a paraphrase of the USSR's rejection of Sweden's protest note following the stranding of the U-137: the Soviet Union was not going to provide assurance that a repetition would not take place.

Some months later, on July 20, 1983, a day after meeting with Palme and two or three days before meeting with Thunborg, Arbatov also appeared before an audience of diplomats at Geneva's Diplomatic Club. On this occasion he stated that "the stranding of the Whisky submarine off Karlskrona was due to navigation failure, and that in the case of the Hårsfjärden events the Swedish government had explained to the USSR that it had not been possible to identify the nationality of the submarines."[72] Because that is clearly the exact opposite of what the Swedish government's protest note to the USSR says, one can either assume that Arbatov presumed his audience to be so ill-informed as not to notice the discrepancy in his remarks or that he was suggesting that he was privately informed by senior members of the Swedish government that Sweden's public statements were false. In a 1986 Swedish television interview Arbatov said that he had personally told Palme that "you cannot consider us such idiots to do these things. We keep 100 kilometers from Sweden's borders."[73]

The domestic political repercussions that followed the disclosure of Ferm's contact with Soviet government representatives can, for the most part, be credited to Prime Minister Palme and can be described as the third of the "neutrality affairs" that took place in 1983 and 1984. (The first of these, the so-called Bahr affair, was unrelated to the Soviet submarine issue. It was disclosed that the West German Social Democratic Party (SPD) politician, Egon Bahr, suggested and wrote the draft of a recommendation in the Palme Commission report for a tactical nuclear-free corridor in the GDR and FRG, which the Swedish foreign ministry subsequently adopted as a Swedish government proposal.)

The second "affair" was called the Bildt affair. On April 28–29, immediately after the public release of the SDC report, Carl Bildt, a member of the commission, traveled to Washington. In a program arranged through the Swedish embassy, he met with various members of the U.S. defense and intelligence community. Such trips are, in fact, routine for members of Sweden's foreign and defense ministries, including those in Social Democratic administrations. Anders Thunborg made the same kind of consultative trip the week before he assumed the office of defense minister in Palme's government, and both Bildt and Thunborg made another more or less similar trip together in April 1985.

Palme disclosed the trip on May 20, however, together

with a sharp attack on Bildt, in a cabinet declaration. He charged that Bildt's meeting with U.S. defense officials "before the ink had dried on the Commission report, was extremely dangerous for the credibility of Swedish neutrality policy. Bildt's behavior ran a great risk that Swedish security policy would be linked to NATO."[74] Palme would repeatedly return to the theme of the moderates as a danger to Swedish neutrality policy in the coming months, but to add to the irony of Palme's attacks, his emissary, Ferm, was meeting with Milstein, the former GRU official, at the same time Bildt was meeting with the Americans – though this was not known at the time of Palme's remarks. On May 20, Palme twice refused to reply to a question in the parliamentary foreign policy commission as to whether the government had made any private contacts with the Soviet government. Between May 20 and September 1983, Palme did not inform the parliamentary committee of Ferm's contacts with Arbatov and Milstein. Instead, he criticized the reports from the Swedish embassy in Washington regarding Arbatov's Carnegie seminar remarks on the basis of a cable from Ambassador Ferm, who told Palme that Arbatov had not made the alleged comments.

When Ferm's meetings with Milstein and Arbatov were made public in December 1983 through the leak of a portion of Ferm's letter reporting to Palme on his discussions with the two Soviets, it led to the third and most serious "affair." The conservative newspaper *Svenska Dagbladet* charged that Palme was delivering a double message to the USSR: a strong line in public and a softer one in private. As best as is known, at least from the public reports of Ferm's meetings, this was not in fact the case, although Ferm had reportedly expressed skepticism to his colleagues about the conclusions in the SDC's report regarding the identification of the submarine's nationality. Ferm's letter had not been registered in the government's archives by Palme, nor had it gone to the foreign ministry in the routine manner. Palme was thus forced to register the letter in the archives and defend his emissary in public. He did this by reading what he claimed to be the full contents of the letter on television. When the letter's complete text was finally leaked in May 1984, it developed that Palme had in fact omitted reading about half of its contents. These included some remarks by Milstein that might have been construed as mildly embarrassing to Sweden – that Sweden was a country of marginal importance for the USSR and that the USSR has more important criteria on which to base its decisions. More important, however, he had also omitted reading two crucial portions: Milstein's comments that the conversations and Palme's message would "have an effect in Moscow, perhaps not immediately. . . ." and that "the USSR would not admit to any territorial violations even if the evidence were indisputable."[75]

Ferm had also written a cable back to Palme saying "that he would be very disappointed if Arbatov had lied and asked him to convey untruthful information to Olof Palme."[76] Arbatov's message was obviously the same one he has claimed to have given Palme personally. The problem that faced both Palme and Ferm is a simple human problem that is easily understood: it was difficult for them to believe that a man with whom they had worked for three years and with whom they would be continuing to work would lie directly to them, even in the service of his state. Besides that difficulty, accepting Arbatov's prediction that the submarine incursions would continue had devastating implications for Palme's hopes for his entire foreign policy program. Palme responded by launching a vicious attack on the Moderate Party, which he said was as important to "ward off" as were the territorial violations by foreign submarines. Palme consistently tried to turn any criticism of his policies into a countercharge that his critics – the opposition party – endangered Swedish neutrality. He also was acerbic about leaks in the foreign ministry and, allegedly, the parliamentary Foreign Affairs Committee, which had put some of this information before the public.

The Soviet response to the commission's report, the Swedish government's protest note, and Palme's private message with its three points was again definitive and, in this case, immediate. Within a week another combined submarine operation – using full-sized submarines and midget submarines – was begun inside Sundsvall harbor, deep within Sweden's internal waters. The submarine incursions in Norway's Hardangerfjord also began within 24 hours of the release of the commission's report. Even in the week preceding the release of the report, around April 20, an unidentified submarine had penetrated Swedish waters south of Ronneby during another set of Swedish weapons tests. The publicized submarine incursions in the spring and summer of 1983 were as follows:

- April 20: South of Ronneby
- April 24: Nämndöfjärden (near Muskö naval base)
- May 1–10: Sundsvall; two submarines and one or more midget submarines
- May 9: South of Muskö naval base
- July 17: Sundsvall
- July 29–August 2: Töre
- End August–September: Karlskrona; major ASW operations lasting nearly a month

In several of these events (Ronneby and Muskö), the submarine's conning tower was reportedly partly visible for some time. Detection of both submarines and midget submarines in various instances was provided by active and passive hydrophones, magnetic-anomaly instrumentation, and radar Elint.[77] ASW operations were carried out in three of the events to attempt to force the submarine to the surface: in Sundsvall, Töre, and Karlskrona. Depth charges were used in all three events, as well as mines in the Sundsvall operations. In Sundsvall, a periscope could be followed in one instance by military personnel, and in another case acoustic signatures were recorded.[78] The submarine passed through two mine fields without detonation taking place upon indications. Although the new IKFN regulations were again applied (before July 1, 1983) and weapons use involved two mines and several depth charges, other aspects of the ASW operations were questionable. Within a day or two after Swedish naval sources stated that no large surface vessels would be permitted in or out of the harbor area before the ASW operations were completed, a large Soviet methanol tanker was permitted to enter on May 7 and to leave on May 8, as were large Finnish Baltic ferries. (A traditional means of submarine or midget submarine escape is to hide under a large boat leaving a guarded area.) The Karlskrona ASW operations received virtually no publicity, in contrast to those in Sundsvall, but were apparently nearly as extensive.

Later in 1983 more events were reported. New bottom tracks were found in the Stockholm archipelago. Divers were observed at a mine chain in the northern Stockholm archipelago. (In 1985 it was disclosed that three mines had been stolen from mine chains, in 1976, 1983 – at another location – and in the fall of 1984.) A submarine was within the exercise area during the Swedish east coast maneuvers on September 22–October 3, and there were additional incidents in mid-September, outside Söderhamn and on September 17, outside Hudiksvall. Depth charges were used in these last two events.

The total number of submarine intrusions in 1983 was 25 certain and 38 probable, much the same as in 1982. Despite this, the Swedish government stated that it could not specify the nationality of any of these intruding submarines or midget submarines.[79] In practical terms this seemed embarrassingly close to a contradiction. If the government admitted that extensive violations were taking place, but that the transgressing submarines could no longer be identified, whose were they supposed to be? Had a different nation suddenly initiated the same kind of operational programs that the Swedish government had previously accused the USSR of carrying out? Was there any reason to doubt the previous identifications? This essentially untenable position was nevertheless maintained for the next two years by the Swedish government. In early 1984 government officials began to claim there were not even "indications" – aside from the question of national identification – during the most extensive episode of all, while Swedish navy and defense spokesmen were publicly releasing sonar recordings and routes taken by an intruding submarine. When it came to the question of "evidence," the Swedish government appeared to believe that only a piece of the submarine would do, while technical evidence such as electronic or acoustical signatures or, more particularly, a combination of such evidence, would not do.

In 1983 submarines had been visible at times during the intrusions, had penetrated Swedish security zones and major naval base areas and had even done so during exercises and maneuvers. Nevertheless, after the Swedish government's official protest note to the USSR and Palme's three-point message to the Soviet political leadership, both of which insisted that the USSR stop the submarine intrusions, the Swedish government could not bring itself to say publicly that the USSR continued to do as it pleased in Swedish territorial waters. The USSR had called Palme's bluff within a matter of days about the possibility of actually sinking a submarine, and it continued to do so all year.

The USSR had also quickly replied to the Swedish government's protest note in another way – with a note of rejection, but requesting the Swedish government not make the note public, and the government had not even shown it to the opposition parties. Then on May 6, in the middle of the Sundsvall incursions, the USSR itself publicly released the rejection. The reply stated that the Swedish note,

> which is totally divorced from reality, is considered by the Soviet Union as an unfriendly act.
>
> According to precise and carefully verified information from the relevant Soviet authorities, Soviet submarines were not in Swedish territorial waters at the time given in the note; nor did they come within 30 km. of these waters. For this very reason they could not

have carried out the activities described in the Swedish government's note. . . .

It ought to be well known to the Swedish government that the Soviet Union has always acted on the basis of a strict adherence to the recognized rules of international law regarding respect for the territorial boundaries of other states.

The untenable claims made in its statement— whether intended or not from the Swedish side— . . . are directed at undermining good neighborly relations with the Soviet Union. . . .

Sweden has taken upon itself the ugly role of spreading fabrications about the Soviet Union and has become involved in a campaign designed to cast suspicions on the USSR's peaceful foreign policy. Such being the case, the baseless claims of the Swedish government as well as statements by officials only supply grist to the mills of those who have developed a massive public offensive against détente and are exploited for the elaboration of a provocative propaganda campaign which has nothing to do with strengthening the cause of peace and which has as its purpose the artificial fostering of distrust among states. . . .

The government of the USSR constantly seeks to develop good neighborly relations with Sweden in a spirit of mutual respect and understanding.[80]

Palme expressed himself as "extraordinarily dissatisfied with the reply to our protest." The Social Democratic government did not, however, publish the Soviet rejection note in its annual compilation of government documents. On June 3, an *Izvestia* article offered the Swedish government advice that had multiple possible interpretations:

It is necessary to seriously pose the question: do the participants in the practical joke have the slightest understanding of where the boundary between reality and fantasy lies. . . . It is regrettable that responsible Swed-

ish political circles haven't yet succeeded in understanding the submarine stories and on realistic
grounds draw the correct conclusions.[81]

The USSR also requested that the Swedish government
punish those responsible for the submarine commission's
report and proposed a joint Soviet-Swedish commission to
review the evidence.[82] The Swedish government explicitly
rejected the second suggestion, but as part of its reply
turned over to the USSR several tapes of technical evidence. It claimed that these did not contain more information than had been made public in the commission's report,
but it refused to release the tapes in Sweden, thus raising
questions about their contents.[83]

Soviet Reaction

While surveying the sequence of the submarine incursions
into Swedish waters and the domestic political problems
that they produced in Sweden, it is also useful to indicate
the Soviet portrayal of the events and the charges that were
made against the USSR. It helps the observer place in context the subsequent interaction between the Soviet and
Swedish governments as well as the continuing intrusions as
they were taking place. For this reason, this material has been
placed here rather than in the discussion of Soviet policy in
chapter 4. In addition Soviet press commentary on both the
Hårsfjärden events and the Swedish submarine commission
report is extremely interesting as a source of insight into the
relation between Soviet information policy and foreign policy
interests. Some examples of these comments for Soviet and
for foreign audiences are presented below.

• "In the early 1970s with a prompting from the CIA
Norway faked up a propaganda story alleging that unidentified, that is Soviet, submarines regularly entered Norwegian fjords. . . . It is highly significant that the hullaballo
about mythical Soviet submarines was raised whenever a

new defense budget was tabled for discussion." The article goes on to claim that a Swedish naval captain, Nils Bruselius, wrote an article in *Marin Nytt* in which he claimed that "the submarine in Hårsfjärden belonged to one of the NATO member countries."[84] The article says nothing of the sort. The author in fact claims that the intruding submarines were Soviet and were letting themselves be observed on purpose. The Soviet commentary ends with the sentence: "Sweden figures prominently in the NATO plans of such (a nuclear-missile) war."[85]

• Another report claimed that the allegations of Soviet submarines in Swedish waters was a myth, as well as part of an unseemly anti-Soviet campaign, of which the Swedish Submarine Commission was a part. It repeated portions of the Soviet note of rejection and added, "Who benefits from the slanderous campaign about the Soviet submarines launched in Sweden? Those who have long been trying to disrupt the process of détente. [It is] another in an attempt to smear the USSR's peaceful foreign policy and undermine its good relations with Sweden."[86]

• "The Soviet government has definitively explained that there are forces not only in Sweden, but outside its borders, that lie behind the campaign of lies about Soviet submarines." This article then offers a new disclosure, which it says the Swedish media know about but will not mention, and which is repeated in numerous of the other stories – that there is a pathway within Swedish territorial waters for NATO submarines and that any NATO submarine found there is allowed to leave freely. This was also contrived from Bruselius' *Marin Nytt* article – which says nothing of the sort.[87] Another article quotes the Swedish *Dagens Industri* and refers to "well informed Swedish and foreign military sources" that asserted that "special noise-catching devices" determined the submarine to be NATO's.[88]

• Another report argued that the accusations are entirely absurd because the Swedes themselves provide detailed coastal maps and submarines do not have to go to test the area. "The USSR has always operated on the principles of strict adherence to the generally accepted norms of international law and respect for other nations' borders. The provocative propaganda campaign which in part is based on manipulated and falsified material is presently led by the Pentagon and certain NATO circles that use the Swedish press as a mouthpiece."[89]

- "Back in the fall of last year it was stated publicly and authoritatively on the Soviet side that no Soviet submarines have been and could not be in the area of Stockholm skerries. One wonders about the purpose of repeating over and over again inventions already disproved. One is inclined to conclude that the anti-Soviet campaign around the mythical 'violations' is designed to prejudice relations between the two countries. Besides, and this leaps to the eye, it aims at obtaining additional allocations on armaments. Certain quarters both in Sweden and elsewhere are interested in both."[90]

- "Certain circles in Sweden as well as outside that country do not stop their assiduous campaign around the controversial report by the Swedish government's commission, which tried to prove that Soviet submarines violated Sweden's territorial waters but failed to produce any direct evidence to corroborate the inventions for the sole reason that none exists. . . .

"It is apparently believed in these circles that the spy scare may divert people away from the urgent problem of how to save Europe from the American plans to saturate it with nuclear weapons and involve Western European countries into the dangerous arms race. . . .

"The commission's report itself is not far from this provocative campaign. It is no accident that sensible assessment does occur in the Swedish press. It is noted, for instance, that the report was inspired by right-wing militarist circles which seek to disrupt the anti-war movement and undermine Sweden's policy of non-participation in military blocs. It is no secret that the United States is striving to involve Sweden in one way or another into the military

NATO bloc—the fact acknowledged by the Western Press.

"It is the undeniable truth that it is in the interests of all countries to develop normal business relations, rather than resort to propaganda based on dubious 'data' and fabrications used to corroborate the allegations that Sweden's territorial waters teem with Soviet submarines.

"It should be clearly stated once again that the Soviet Union firmly sticks to international commitments and accords and observes the principle of inviolability and respect of borders. As to those who declare that they can determine by dubious 'imprints on the seabed' that such 'violations' take place, it is quite obvious that they are guided by other premeditated goals—those of complicating Soviet-Swedish relations and aggravating the situation in Northern Europe."[91]

1984

The political crux of the submarine intrusions and Swedish-Soviet relations took place early in 1984. Sometime in the summer of 1983, Prime Minister Palme and Swedish Foreign Minister Lennart Bodström had both received messages from Soviet leader Juri Andropov, transmitted via Finland's President Mauno Koivisto, to the effect that no Soviet submarines had violated Swedish waters since the U-137 grounding in 1981.[92] The Soviet message repeated the portions of the Soviet rejection note claiming that no Soviet submarines had been in Hårsfjärden and that all Soviet submarines have a standing order not to come any closer than 30 km to the Swedish maritime territorial border. The same message was again given to a senior Swedish foreign ministry official on a visit to Moscow early in March 1984—in the middle of the next major series of violations.[93] In October 1983, Palme had stated that exchanges with the USSR at the ministerial level could not be resumed until it was clear that the USSR respected Sweden's neutrality and territorial integrity, that is, until it was clear that the submarine intrusions had stopped. In January, Soviet Foreign Minister Gromyko was expected in Stockholm for the opening of the Stockholm Conference – the Conference on Confidence and Security-Building and Disarmament (CDE) in Europe. It had been announced in advance that Gromyko would meet with Palme while he was in Stockholm and that the Soviet submarine intrusions would be a subject for their discussions. By January 1984, the Swedish government had also decided to resume ministerial visits after Gromyko's trip to Stockholm.[94]

After the meeting between Palme and Gromyko, the prime minister informed the Swedish press that

> The Soviet Union's highest leadership has promised to respect Sweden's neutrality and territorial integrity. . . . Sweden has, through Andrej Gromyko, now obtained notice from the Soviet Union's highest leadership that Swedish neutrality is respected and that it is understood that submarine intrusions cannot be tolerated.[94]

Palme added that "Sweden would combat violations with all strength. If submarines from foreign nations violate Swedish waters, Sweden will attack them. Sooner or later we will succeed in damaging or sinking a foreign submarine." On the following day, the Swedish foreign minister in the preceding nonsocialist government, Ola Ullsten, publicly noted that Gromyko had promised exactly the same thing when they had met in New York shortly after the stranding of the Soviet submarine in October 1981.[96] This information, which must have been on record in the foreign ministry, received no comment from the government. Neither was it denied.

After also meeting with Gromyko during his January visit and without directly discussing submarine intrusions, Swedish Foreign Minister Bodström proclaimed that "there was no doubt that the USSR respects Sweden's neutrality."[97] Three months later, after the longest of all the submarine intrusion sequences, Bodström alleged that "the Soviet

Union has no other interests in Northern Europe than friendly relations with Sweden and the other Nordic countries," and that "the Swedish government places great weight on the assurances that Foreign Minister Gromyko made that the USSR has not violated Swedish territory since the grounding in Gåsfjärden in 1981."[98] With this remark Foreign Minister Bodström seemingly undercut his own government's position, which identified the USSR as responsible for the October 1982 events.

It developed, however, that Gromyko had said little or nothing that was attributed to him in the press reports published at the time of his meeting with Prime Minister Palme, which were a direct result of Palme's description of the conversation. Palme has gratuitously formulated an alleged Soviet reply to his three points. What little Gromyko said on the subject closely paralleled portions of the Soviet May 1983 note of rejection, which Palme had previously said the Swedish government found unsatisfactory. During their conversations, it was Palme – and not Gromyko – who noted that the Soviet government had said that it respected Swedish neutrality and territorial integrity. Sweden wanted to provide a concrete form to such expressions and on that basis develop Swedish-Soviet relations. Sweden desired good relations with the USSR, and the Swedish government noted that the USSR had expressed a reciprocal wish.[99] Gromyko reportedly replied by asking "what kind of dragons the Swedes actually saw out in the Baltic." Palme pointed out that the Swedish reports on the submarine violations in the fall of 1983 had not attributed them to any particular state. Gromyko's only other relevant comment was that "the USSR had no cause to be active in Swedish waters, and therefore the question should not be discussed any further." There was apparently no specific mention by either party of the Hårsfjärden events or the Swedish protest note. Instead, Gromyko criticized the Swedish government for not having made sufficient efforts to improve relations with the USSR in the preceding months and for not doing more to further the idea of a Nordic Nuclear-Free

Zone. Palme subsequently claimed that the disclosures from leaked foreign ministry summaries of the conversations provided "an incomplete picture" and might give "a mistaken impression."

> I conveyed to Gromyko, with all the desired exactness, the Swedish government's clear attitude concerning the protection of our territorial integrity. I also said that we will react to encroachments on our territory with full political and military force. There will be no deviation from the Swedish policy of neutrality.[100]

The foreign ministry's press spokesman added that the disclosure of classified materials could seriously damage Sweden's diplomatic reliability.

The Swedish newspaper headlines at the time of the Palme-Gromyko meetings in January had said what Palme had wanted them to say — not what Gromyko had said. In an October 1983 interview, Palme had already used phrases similar to those that were attributed to Gromyko after their January 1984 meeting: "The Soviet Union has promised to show us respect . . . has made clear that it intends to respect our neutrality policy."[101] The phrases were creative transformations of portions of the two Soviet rejection notes and must be considered gratuitous interpretations of Soviet government policy. In the same interview, in other phrases whose significance was totally overlooked at the time, Palme also said that it could not be absolutely certain that submarine violations continued after Hårsfjärden — more carefully qualified but essentially the same remarks as those of Foreign Minister Bodström in February 1985, which would bring on a political crisis.

On February 9, less than a month after the Palme-Gromyko meeting and the supposed assurances of Soviet respect for Swedish territorial integrity, the longest and most embarrassing of all the submarine incursion incidents be-

gan. It lasted just over 30 days and took place directly in
Karlskrona harbor – Sweden's second largest naval base,
only several months after the previous ASW operation in
the harbor, in September 1983. The area is an enclosed basin of 5 by 15 km, and the entrance and exit passages can
more easily be closed. The initial indications came from
bottom-mounted magnetic anomaly detectors. Acoustic recordings and radar as well as visual observations were the
additional observation sources.[102] Some newly acquired
equipment was used for the first time: buoy-mounted hydrophones and high frequency sonars, including one or
more mine sweepers equipped with high frequency sonars.
The latter had reportedly been under test since the middle
of 1983.

The intruding unit involved three submarines (two outside the basin barriers), midget submarines, and this time
also small, motorized diver vehicles and visible diver activity. Weapons expenditure was substantial: 1 mine and 22
depth charges (all on February 14), but also 28 substrength
warning munitions. Depth charges were still used "for the
purpose of warning," which was no longer necessary in internal waters according to the new IKFN regulations. Orders
were presumably the same as they had been before: force
the intruding units to the surface. Although practices could
in effect be the same, the emphasis was not on attacking
the vehicles directly. Not only did no "orders to sink the
vessels . . . come promptly from Stockholm," it would also
appear that they may have been watered down still further:
"The primary aim for the submarine defense measures is to
increase the risk for an intruder so much that he doesn't
find it profitable to continue. . . . We have demonstrated so
determined a will to put an end to the violations that they
should effect the intruder's risk calculations."[103] There was
no mention of "damage," or "destroy." The submarine outside
the encircled basin entrance was only to be warned off, although it was also well within the area in which the new
IKFN regulations directed that submarines should be
forced to the surface. Some days into the ASW operations

the restrictions regarding the area just outside the enclosed basin were reportedly withdrawn.

The government clearly tried to distance itself from the ASW operations as much as possible. There was no comment on the events from anyone in the government for more than 20 days, and at the height of the incident the prime minister went on a skiing holiday and the foreign and defense ministers were both away from Stockholm. Unidentified members of Palme's staff claimed that they were skeptical that there was evidence for anything at all being present in the area. The navy replied by releasing a detailed plot of one episode in which a submarine was followed for some 30 minutes. During this time, it passed over a MAD line on two occasions and was in effect warned away from passing over an allegedly operating mine line by the use of a helicopter dipping sonar. The submarine was not attacked during that interval.

When directly asked on the twenty-eighth day whether the military had permission to attack the submarine, Palme replied: "We have cleared that up now." Exactly what that meant was never explained, though it would not appear to be a clear "yes." In the same television interview, Palme explained that during the Sundsvall ASW operations in 1983 it had taken only eight minutes for him to receive and reply to a message from the field via the commander in chief and minister of defense and he thought "that wasn't bad." (In eight minutes, a submarine could move three-quarters to one and one-half miles, depending on its underwater speed.) Although communications between the prime minister's office and the military command were visibly poor — with Palme commenting about the evidence being inadequate and having been misunderstood by the military command — he reportedly had not interfered in the Karlskrona operations. The commander in chief said that "no limiting restrictions existed" other than those concerning the safety of one's own personnel and the civilian community.[104] The head of the navy also claimed that none of the preceding five governments had ever placed any restrictions on him other than those in the IKFN regulations.[105]

Following the unsuccessful conclusion of the Karlskrona ASW operations, Swedish military authorities made a number of significant comments. The official reports of the commander in chief were again critical of excessive confusion and misjudgments. Vice Admiral Bengt Schuback, who had led the operations in Karlskrona and who was to become the new head of the navy on October 1, suggested that some of the smaller intruding underwater vehicles had been nonmagnetic. New technology made it possible for a midget submarine to cross the entire Baltic without a mother vessel. Because this came close to implying the national identity of the intruding vehicles, Schuback remarked that "I have a personal and very clear understanding of where the vehicles and divers come from. I cannot, however, provide details for that in my official capacity."[106] He believed that it was impossible to protect the entire Swedish coast, but that he hoped that at least the three or four most important zones could be protected. He also hoped that this could be done by stopping the submarines farther out in territorial waters: the lesson of the Karlskrona operations was that the ASW forces would have to react more quickly.

The chief of the Defense staff took up the same theme in mid-1985: Swedish military forces would react more quickly on any subsequent occasion.[107] Commercial boat traffic would be stopped in the future during ASW operations at Karlskrona and Muskö and within one to two years permanent barriers composed of hydrophones, other fixed sensors, and mines would be available to prevent both submarines and midget submarines from getting into the two base areas.[108] During the February–March Karlskrona ASW operations, the Defense staff had said that no boats would enter Karlskrona harbor until the operations were completed. Nevertheless, large civilian ships could leave and enter the basin freely until February 20; although regulated after that, some large vessels were still permitted to enter and leave the area.

In the spring of 1984, the government considered whether to introduce the issue of the submarine violations of Swedish internal waters at the CDE.[109] It unquestionably would have been an appropriate subject, but nevertheless, the issue was not raised in any direct or significant fashion. Sweden's under secretary of state limited himself to an oblique reference to territorial integrity and the problems of the Baltic in a speech to the conference in June 1984. More remarkable still was a change in the phrasing used by the government in referring to the submarine incursions. The report on incidents that took place in the fall of 1983 was released by the commander in chief late in December 1983. It referred to three "clear cases" of submarine violations and new bottom tracks that had been found. The defense minister used the same phrases in a statement that accompanied the release. The prime minister and the foreign minister made no comment. The government's foreign policy declaration in parliament three months later, on March 21, 1984, referred only to "a number of observations in which the responsible authorities could not rule out that there was a question of purposeful penetrations of Swedish territory." The phrasing was similar to the convoluted phrasing Palme had used in his October 3, 1983 interview.[110] Only a single newspaper editorial and the conservative party's defense specialist, Bildt, commented on the oblique and confusing language or its implications.[111]

Submarine incursions continued through the remainder of 1984.[112] The language in the commander in chief's quarterly and annual reports also became more diffuse, and one of the categories of submarine violations was omitted from the reports. The Defense staff also claimed that it did not want to report "where, when, or the precise number of the violations that have occurred" so as not to give those responsible for the submarine violations knowledge of Swedish detection capabilities.[113] A third set of bottom tracks dating from the fall of 1984 were found in the spring of

1985, but their discovery was not disclosed in subsequent quarterly reports, although the head of the navy claimed that the government had imposed no political restrictions to the reporting of submarine violations.[114] If that is correct then the military was itself responsible for the more restrictive policy.

Aircraft Violations

At the peak of public indignation at the submarine violations, Swedish Foreign Minister Bodström had urged that Sweden make a more serious issue of aircraft violations and publicize each of these events. (Bodström had also stated that Sweden "would sink" intruding submarines.) The majority of the violations of Swedish territorial airspace are routinely made by NATO aircraft. The Baltic is an area of substantial aerial reconnaissance traffic: The United States has flown P-3 Orion and SR-71 aircraft regularly; Great Britain, Nimrod; West Germany, Breuget Atlantic; Sweden itself, Caravelles; and the USSR, several types of maritime reconnaissance aircraft. All of these remain in international airspace in the great majority of cases. Ground-based aircraft of Sweden or the USSR frequently take off to inspect the reconnaissance aircraft flying past. At one point between the island of Gotland and the Swedish mainland, there is only a narrow international airspace passage four km wide. Six different nations use the Baltic airspace as an exercise area, yet incursions are relatively rare, which indicates that care is ordinarily taken. In the case of territorial air violations in which the nationality of the intruding aircraft is identified, the Swedish foreign ministry routinely files a protest.

On August 9, 1984, a Suchoi SU-15 interceptor aircraft participating in a Soviet air defense exercise in the Baltic followed a Swedish civilian airliner into Swedish territory over the island of Gotland for several minutes.[115] The Swedish aircraft had passed through Polish airspace and was flying over the dead center of the Baltic. The area in which this violation occurred was in full view of both Swedish and Soviet ground-based radars. Swedish military authorities could identify the specific aircraft that was involved. Soviet pilots in this and other incidents described do not engage in low altitude incursions under radar: they are under control of their own ground-based radar at all times. Sweden had no interceptor aircraft based on Gotland for some years. The Swedish government did not, however, make the incident public until it had been leaked to the press two weeks later, on August 25. After a month's delay, Sweden released minute-by-minute time and location maps of the two aircraft over the Baltic.[116] The Soviet interceptor had spent four and a half minutes inside Swedish airspace and did not turn until it had flown over and along the coast of Gotland for about a minute.

The most important aspect of the incident probably was the sequence of events concerning the official Swedish protest. The Swedish protest was oral, but included a somewhat unconventional aide-mémoire by way of "a reminder." According to protocol, this is less than a protest note. The USSR rejected the Swedish protest as groundless. When Sweden resubmitted it, it was rejected a second time. The Soviet oral rejections briefly stated that the competent Soviet authorities could not confirm the Swedish allegation and therefore rejected it. The Swedish foreign ministry interpreted this as less of an absolute denial than the Soviet rejection of the Hårsfjärden submarine events had been, but the difference does not seem to be significant. Swedish diplomatic sources reportedly interpreted the phrasing in the first Soviet rejection on September 4 as an indication that the USSR might acknowledge the infraction if Sweden released its evidence. Sweden did so on September 7, but the Soviets rejected the second protest just the same. The spokesman of the Soviet foreign ministry, Vladimir Lomejko, suggested that it would be more appropriate if Sweden investigated all the known cases of NATO violations of Swedish territory at sea and in the air. A month or so after

the second Soviet rejection, Vadim Zagladin, deputy director of the International Department of the Central Committee, showed a visiting Swedish journalist a map that pur-
ported to prove the Soviet statement regarding the location
of their aircraft.[117] The map was an obvious attempt at disinformation and had not been shown to two Swedish government ministers who had visited the USSR only a few
days before and had raised the issue of the aircraft incursion. They were instead assured by their counterparts and
by Deputy Chairman of the USSR Council of Ministers
Gejdar Aliyev that the USSR fully respects Swedish neutrality and territorial integrity.[118] Swedish Defense officials
explained that the Soviet aircraft's ability to penetrate
Swedish airspace was due to Swedish problems in maintaining readiness. There was one other unusual violation in
1984, in which a Polish military aircraft violated Swedish
airspace south of Karlskrona on four occasions in immediate succession, each time after being warned off by Swedish
interceptor aircraft.

The remaining major air incursion took place on June
26, 1985. A Soviet TU-16 Badger medium bomber flew on a
direct course from Soviet territory toward Gotland. It was
over Swedish airspace for three and a half minutes. Swedish
interceptors were scrambled, at which point the Soviet aircraft reversed its course. The Swedish aircraft did not reach
the bomber until it was again in international airspace, but
they photographed it. The Swedish foreign ministry made a
low-level, oral comment to the USSR on July 5, but did not
make the event public until it was again leaked to the press
on September 3.

In October 1984, the foreign ministry had announced
that a change in procedures on disclosure of information
would include the reporting of "serious individual incidents"
and the government response. The June 1985 bomber incursion was, however, reportedly not classified as a serious
event by either the Defense or Foreign Ministries.[119] The
foreign ministry apparently anticipated a Soviet acknowl-

edgement, because relations between the USSR and Sweden had by this time been normalized. On August 16, the
USSR, however, rejected the Swedish July comment. Sweden repeated the protest, now as a reminder (or "admonition, objection"), adding additional evidence, and on September 20 the USSR orally acknowledged the violation and
regretted that it had taken place.[120]

On none of these occasions would the Swedish government even remotely have considered shooting down Soviet
military aircraft intruding over Swedish borders in peacetime despite the public statement by Soviet Chief of Staff
Nikolai Ogarkov in 1984 that this was the right of every
nation, even in the case of civilian aircraft. (In June 1952
the USSR had shot down two Swedish reconnaissance aircraft in international waters in the Baltic. The events took
place close to the Swedish island of Gotland and not near
Soviet territorial airspace. Nevertheless the USSR claimed
that the Swedish aircraft had violated Soviet airspace and
that "to defend the Soviet borders is a responsibility and a
necessity for the Soviet state.")[121]

Soviet Reaction

Soviet commentary in 1984 on the submarine intrusions and
on Soviet-Swedish relations included several notable differ-
ences and initiatives. Most of these occurred in March 1984
just as the month-long ASW operations in Karlskrona,
which had been the most extensive to date, came to an end.
On March 15, 1984, the Soviet Foreign Ministry sent a tele-
gram to Sweden in commemoration of the sixtieth anniversary of USSR-Swedish diplomatic relations:

> Unquestionable advances in the development of multi-
> faceted cooperation between our countries has been
> achieved in the preceding period. Today, in conditions
> of a seriously deteriorating international situation, and
> of the increased threat of war on the European conti-
> nent, it would be particularly urgent to observe the

continued development of relations on the basis of realism, in a spirit of trust and mutual understanding.[122]

The expressed hope for greater realism in Swedish attitudes
in the future seems a distinct repetition of the June 1983
Izvestia comment that Swedish authorities had not yet
drawn the appropriate realistic conclusions from the allegedly nonexistent incidents. Soviet diplomacy has often
used the term realism to indicate a Western accommodation
to Soviet policy interests. For example, during the period of
détente, Soviet spokesmen repeatedly noted that certain
Western leaders were "realistic" enough to accommodate to
the fact of Soviet power.

On the same day *Pravda* commented:

> Since the very establishment of Soviet-Swedish diplomat-
> ic relations it has become obvious that the principled
> policy of peace and peaceful coexistence, which is being
> consistently implemented by the Soviet Union, is en-
> thusiastically welcomed by the peace-loving Swedish
> people.

A long section followed, praising Prime Minister Palme personally and the Swedish government's policies on a Nordic
Nuclear-Free Zone, a nuclear weapon-free corridor on the
European mainland, and noted that "the Swedish public at
large, and many Swedish officials, have invariably acted
from common sense. . . ." The article then stated that NATO
and the United States

> the foes of Soviet-Swedish good-neighborliness catch
> at any pretext, however absurd and far fetched it may
> be, such as the allegation about Soviet submarines de-
> liberately penetrating Swedish territorial waters, in or-
> der to cause hostility in Sweden with respect to the
> USSR and to cast a shadow at the USSR's peace loving
> policy.[123]

The Soviet Union returned to the first of these themes again in 1985 in publications intended for international audiences.

> Ever since diplomatic relations were established between the Soviet Union and Sweden in 1924, the Soviet government has firmly and consistently explained that it respects the Swedish policy of neutrality and is prepared to develop interstate and other relations on the basis of mutual advantage. Practical behavior from the Soviet side has followed the same principles. . . .
>
> The Soviet Union has on repeated occasions declared that it wishes a comprehensive and multifaceted cooperation with its neighbor Sweden, and shows in its acts its respect for [Sweden's] traditional neutral policy. Because of its natural wish to live in peace and harmony with its neighbors and other people, the Soviet Union strictly follows the basic principles of international law — respect for each others' sovereignty, and nonintervention in each other's internal affairs.[124]

Again the report noted that after periods of chilled relations "good sense in the end always took over."

In the second Soviet initiative, the Soviet ambassador in Stockholm spent the month of March in informal conversations with members of the Swedish government, parliament, and opposition parties discussing the submarine violations. Prime Minister Palme noted once again that the national identity of the submarines in Karlskrona could not be determined. The Soviet ambassador invited the Speaker of the Swedish Parliament to visit Moscow as the head of a parliamentary delegation.[125] According to Swedish constitutional law, the Speaker of the Parliament is the highest representative of the Swedish state following the king. The invitation therefore had greater implications than are immediately apparent and indicated Soviet interest in accelerating the "normalization" of relations between the two states — as the submarine operations continued.

The third Soviet initiative took place because of an opportunity provided by Sweden. Alexander Bovin, a former Central Committee staff member and well-known political columnist for *Izvestia*, had been invited to Sweden by the foreign ministry in the hope that he might report home on the tenor of Swedish feelings about the submarine intrusions. Instead he went on the attack, much in the manner of Foreign Minister Gromyko two months previously. His theme, first introduced in an *Izvestia* editorial in May 1983, was a rhetorical question: "Who benefits by poor Swedish-Soviet relations?" Obviously only the United States, NATO, and "the enemies of peace." Because it was unquestionably Sweden that was making accusations – of which the USSR was innocent – Sweden was responsible for the unsatisfactory situation and for the deterioration of relations.

At the same time, Bovin's widely noted article in the Swedish press in March 1984 contained a hint that there were indeed Soviet submarine operations. He explained that "the increase in the general international level of tension and among other things the intensification of NATO's activities in North Europe and in the Baltic area naturally force the Warsaw Pact to provide for its security. That increases the likelihood of undesirable incidents."[126] He accompanied this with the admonition that "good relations between states require a mutual understanding not only on the government level but also at other levels" and specifically urged the Swedish government to muzzle both its military and the journalistic profession on the subject of submarine incidents.

The Swedish press had published other such admonitions by major Soviet spokesmen before and would do so again in 1985. For example, the deputy editor of *Izvestia* only a month earlier had charged that "neutral Sweden's press was often more anti-Soviet than the press in NATO countries."[127] In 1985 another invited Soviet columnist explained that "every sound thinking Swedish journalist had to agree that information had to be grounded in facts that corresponded to reality" and that Swedish journalists as well as Soviet ones had a special responsibility to develop good neighborly relations between the two countries.[128]

Following the Karlskrona ASW operations the Soviet press again also published a number of commentaries of the sort that had been published in 1983. *Krasnaya Zvezda's* analysis of the "submarine hallucinations" was that

> It is the desire of the Swedish right wing forces to see alien submarines off the coast of the country that stands behind "periscope disease." These forces are interested in arms buildup, close links with NATO, and in promoting mistrust in the USSR's foreign policy. They want to spoil the traditional good-neighborly relations between the USSR and Sweden and for this purpose they incite anti-Soviet submarine hallucinations. This disease may have extremely bad consequences. They damage not only the neutrality of Sweden, but détente and the strengthening of peace in Northern Europe.[129]

An *Izvestia* article went on to repeat the theme that the "battleship games" were timed by Swedish and Norwegian navies at budget appropriation times so as to obtain greater allocations and ended with noting that the submarine allegations were a symptom "of extreme fits of war jitters" and always resolved themselves into a noisy anti-Soviet campaign."[130] A second article described

> the brazen and malicious anti-Soviet campaign some Swedish bourgeois newspapers have waged for a long time. The opponents of Swedish-Soviet good-neighborliness alleged that Soviet submarines were engaged in unpermitted activities off the Swedish shores. . . .
>
> Right wing elements used such allegations to promote anti-Sovietism apparently to trick the Swedish government into making ill-advised steps with regard to the Soviet Union and to draw Stockholm into the implementation of Washington's militaristic plans in Northern Europe. Undoubtedly another aim of the

campaign was to compromise the idea, popular in Scandinavia, of a nuclear-free zone for Northern Europe.[131]

The article ended with the suggestion that it was U.S. midget submarines that were "on running trials of Sweden and Norway." Several days later, *Pravda* ran the same theme:

> Defense experts in the West have admitted more than once that the Baltic is swarming with submarines from NATO and the United States. . . . It is no accident that [Americans] who want to extract appalling sensations out of the dirty stream of their own anti-Soviet inventions, choose the fjords of the Scandinavian countries as the place for their actions.[132]

1985

The winter of 1984–1985 was cold, and ice conditions in the Baltic and in the archipelagos were the second heaviest since 1900. It was some time before conditions permitted submarine operations relatively close inshore. The year 1985 began with political events. Important voices besides those in the USSR said the submarine intrusions were a mirage from beginning to end. Perhaps the most important of these was Finland's President Mauno Koivisto, who was skeptical of the evidence in the submarine commission's report on the Hårsfjärden events.[133] As late as December 20, 1984, Koivisto offered the opinion that the "submarine intermezzo has . . . for a long time been on the plane of science-fiction novels." He also transmitted the Soviet denials of responsibility for the incidents to Sweden. The Soviets told them

> that if you don't believe us, you might as well not believe us about anything else either. . . . That it is a matter of honor for us . . . that you can be entirely certain. Tell them [the Swedes] that we aren't there and that we don't have any reason to be there.[134]

In his first major foreign policy address in Finland in his three years in office – his New Year's speech to the Finnish nation – only several days before the Soviet cruise missile accident took place in northern Finland, Koivisto proposed a ban on all long-range cruise missiles. On January 7, Koivisto traveled to Stockholm to discuss these questions with Prime Minister Palme.[135] Koivisto was briefed by the Swedish defense minister, and afterward stated that he now believed the SDC report.[136] He was also, however, quoted in a press conference with Finnish journalists as saying that "the Swedish government now had the same understanding [regarding the submarine events] that he always had," which would seem to indicate Koivisto was still skeptical.

Any "advance" in public understanding was quickly reversed by the last and most inflamed of all the "affairs." In a dinner interview with six Swedish journalists early in February 1985, Foreign Minister Bodström stated that no submarine violations had taken place after Hårsfjärden in 1982 and the submarine commission had been unsure of its conclusion that the intruding submarines during the 1982 events were Soviet. The foreign minister also found the Swedish reaction "hysterical" and stated that the Swedish government "assumes that the USSR behaves rationally . . . and could not see any rational explanation as to why the USSR should violate Swedish territorial integrity."[137] Bodström had apparently expressed his doubts on the submarine commission's conclusion as early as September 1983 to the vice chairman of the Parliamentary Foreign Policy Committee. (Bodström had also previously been quoted as saying that he thought that analyzing submarine violations in the foreign ministry was as useful as analyzing dreams.) Former Prime Minister Fälldin demanded Bodström's resignation, and the nonsocialist parties called for a vote of no-confidence in Parliament.[138] Palme, however, rigorously supported his foreign minister, and Bodström claimed that he had only meant that there had been no identification of the USSR as the intruder since 1982.

The government was able to defeat the no-confidence

vote in Parliament, but Palme continued the debate into March and April 1985 with his charges of political "rot" among the opposition. A *Dagens Nyheter* editorial found his line of argument "more than bizarre" and made it clear that the prime minister was attempting to establish the terms of debate by deciding which criticism would be permitted.[139] Palme warned that the foreign interpretation of the Swedish security debate was "dangerous." Unspecified foreign states would expect a change in Swedish security policy if a forthcoming election allowed the conservatives to return to power as part of a nonsocialist government.[140] This harked back to a newspaper interview Palme had given in December 1984 in which he stated that "some quarters in Sweden undermine the conditions for neutrality policy by disclosing their distrust of Soviet attitudes toward our country."[141] Nevertheless, when the Social Democratic Party was reelected in September 1985, Palme named Sten Anderson to replace Foreign Minister Bodström. It is likely that the replacement would have taken place earlier had it been possible to avoid the implication that the nonsocialist parties' criticism regarding his competence had been correct.

By midsummer, indications of submarine activity in 1985 had accumulated and appeared in the commander in chief's quarterly reports. Continuous reconnaissance in both internal and territorial waters was reportedly now maintained, as well as orders to all ship captains and helicopter pilots permitting the use of weapons on indications. Actual ASW operations and indications were reported in

- Göteborg harbor on March 25–28;
- Karlshamn harbor, April 12–13, numerous indications, weapons used;
- Gullmarsfjorden, June 26, indications registered by technical instrumentation;
- reported diver activity at Gålö, near Muskö naval base;
- Öregrund and Gräsö, July 8–11, submarine tower sighted visually;

- Karlskrona harbor area, August 20–23, numerous technical indications; four depth charges used against a suspected submarine and midget submarine;
- Göteborg harbor, August 20–23, submarine tower sighted visually. No ability to investigate because the availability of ASW forces was reportedly not sufficient to carry out operations in more than one area at the same time.

In October, the Defense staff published a brief report that included the first photographs of a small portion of a presumptive midget submarine tower taken in June on the west coast.[142] Better photographs were reportedly not published.

Throughout this period the Swedish government maintained the position that it was impossible to identify the nationality of the intruding submarines, and the opposition nonsocialist parties repeated the same formula. On August 7, during the visit to Stockholm of Soviet Deputy Vice Foreign Minister Victor Maltsev, Swedish-Soviet relations were declared "normalized," and Palme announced that he would travel to Moscow following the fall elections. The Swedish government repeated its formulation that it "fastened upon" Soviet statements of respect for Swedish neutrality and territorial integrity.[143] There was a momentary comic relief episode on the national identification question when Commander in Chief-designate General Bengt Gustafsson remarked in an interview that "I don't understand why the Soviet continues with its submarine violations, but they obviously have unquenchable demands for security for their own country."[144] The Defense staff immediately released a retraction, saying that "Since the incident in Hårsfjärden in the fall of 1982, it has not been possible in any case to specify a particular nation as responsible for the indications of foreign underwater activities that have been reported."[145] General Gustafsson compounded the snafu when he then offered the clarification that the intruding power might be carrying out the submarine penetrations in "a defensive context, to assure themselves that there isn't any threat against them."[146]

The fourth-quarter Defense staff report of submarine activities did not appear until January 1986 and was particularly striking against the background of the government's policies in 1985. There were two larger submarine operations in the fall. The first began in September in the Stockholm archipelago and may have also involved activities near Karlskrona. The second took place in the last week of October and early November, far in the Stockholm archipelago, in the Djurö-Kanholmsfjärden area, and at Oxdjupet, just outside of Vaxholm. One to three submarines are estimated to have been in the area, and the Defense staff report refers to "particularly clear" reports and technically recorded indications of submarine activity.[147] Water temperature was cold and uniform and facilitated sonar sensitivity, and the recordings were reportedly made at a permanently manned site. It was possible to record a submarine's active sonar, and recordings were made of its motor sounds. Naval sources indicated that Whisky submarines had been recorded on the newly acquired sonars, and press reports went so far as to reveal that the recordings strongly indicated double-propellered submarines.[148] The Defense staff nevertheless maintained that the recording quality was not sufficient to establish national identification.[149] No mention was made of weapons use, though news reports indicated that ASW operations had spanned 14 days.

The report argued that "even if the sounds that were recorded together with other indications pointed towards the Warsaw Pact with 100 percent certainty, that was still not sufficient for a Swedish diplomatic action, since identification of the pact is not the same thing as knowing which country within the pact had carried out the violation."[150] When recordings indicated Whisky submarines, a determination between Soviet and Polish submarines had to be made, and opinion was uniform on what that determination meant in reality. The Defense staff was described as having an "operative" assessment that Soviet submarines were responsible for the continued incursions, and the same assessment was made by the Defense Ministry. The newly appointed defense minister, however, commented only that the government viewed the commander in chief's report "with great seriousness," the same formulation his predecessor had used. The major daily – and progovernment – newspaper commented, "In other words, while the government prepares for Olof Palme's visit to Moscow, it is satisfied to assume Swedish waters will continue to be visited by foreign intruders even in the future."[151]

Just as the Bodström affair in the spring of 1985 was a political consequence of the patently contradictory elements in the government's policies, a new round of complications developed in the fall of 1985. This time the political turmoil was produced by the combination of a government formulation and public statements of middle level naval officers involved in ASW operations in the field. National elections had been held in September, and Palme's Social Democratic government had been returned to power. On October 1 the government presented its policy statement at the opening session of the new Parliament. The statement that "we have created respect for our decisiveness to protect our nation's territorial integrity with all the means available" was the only indirect reference to the issue of submarine violations. The analogous government declaration in 1984 had stated "Our territory has suffered violation on numerous occasions."

On October 17, 1985 the commander in chief released the third-quarter report, which referred to continued submarine incursions on the west coast and in the Stockholm archipelago and referred to five particular events. The government's press spokesman claimed that Palme had not known of the contents of the commander in chief's report before it was delivered on October 17.[152] The commander in chief subsequently stated that he had personally informed the government of all "serious" submarine violations since 1980.[153] Several days later, two Swedish naval officers commented on a NATO naval maneuver in the Baltic that included the U.S. battleship *Ohio* and several accompanying vessels, including the *Ticonderoga*, and attributed the NATO naval demonstrations to Sweden's inability to clear its internal and territorial waters of foreign submarines. The relationship may have been extremely indirect at best, given the composition of the NATO exercise force, which was not directed toward ASW, but one of the officers was quoted as saying

> We cannot protect our waters. NATO knows that. Now they are indicating that they aren't going to sit with their arms crossed if the USSR utilizes the Swedish archipelago as a base area in a future crisis situation . . . . Where we don't control the situation foreign powers go in – and prepare for war. We cannot today stop Soviet submarines. . . .
>
> Either we become masters in our own house or we accustom ourselves to being partly occupied – under water."[154]

The officer, a commander of a division of patrol boats in the Karlskrona area, also referred to his contacts with submarines and midget submarines in 1985, which always managed to escape before weapons could be used against them. Admiral Schuback, the head of the navy, reprimanded the two officers. Nevertheless, in the following days, together with Admiral Claes Törnberg, the second ranking naval officer who headed the coastal defense forces, Schuback took several opportunities to state that submarine violations were continuing and that naval resources were not sufficient to defend more than one or two of the four Swedish coastal areas in a time of crisis.[155] By this time the major incidents at the end of October and early November in the Stockholm archipelago would have taken place.

Finally, on November 10, 12 naval field officers publicly criticized the government for toning down the significance and the continuation of the submarine violations and for not being honest with the public.[156] They also stressed that the numbers of submarine incursions were higher in reality than in the numbers presented by the Defense staff, which Admiral Törnberg had also strikingly emphasized by his reference to a 1 percent rate of detection. Palme replied that the remarks of the naval officers were "injudicious," "inappropriate," and "not factual." The government's position was that ASW was being given priority, that the commander in chief and the head of the navy had been given all of the resources and authority that they had requested, and that the government had not restricted the information that the Defense staff could release to the public.[157] In addition, in defending himself against the accusation that the government had toned down the violations, Palme noted that "I have taken up the violations in the United Nations for the first time in the fall." Palme was referring to his speech to the United Nations General Assembly on the occasion of the UN's fortieth anniversary. The sentences in that speech that alluded indirectly to the submarine violations read as follows:

> The rule of law is of vital importance to peaceful international relations. In particular, this is strongly felt in smaller countries. When the integrity and independence of one small country is violated, it sends a vibration of anger and anxiety through the hearts and minds of citizens in other small countries. For them, the rule of law and the observance of our common commitments under the Charter are seen as imperatives of a future in peace and security.
>
> My own country has experienced serious violations of its territorial integrity. To us this has brought home the seriousness of breaches of international law.[158]

One other aspect of the submarine violations developed into a public controversy in 1985. As early as 1981 the head of the Swedish army had published a brief admonition, warning of the possibility of surprise attack, though his conclusions at the time did not seem to have any relation to the submarine incursions.[159] By 1985, however, the term

"Spetsnaz," referring to Soviet elite diversionary and sabotage units, was commonly known. A brigade of these units was allegedly associated with the Baltic Fleet and with each of the 4 Soviet fleets and 16 Front commands.[160] Such units had been used in the Soviet attack on Manchuria in August 1945 and are identified in the 1977 edition of the *Soviet Military Encyclopedia*. They began to be referred to in relation to the midget submarines.

In 1985 the Swedish army journal published two articles on foreign sabotage units and noted that Sweden had to anticipate attack by such forces in advance of a major full-scale invasion or a surprise attack. The articles never once referred specifically to the Soviet Union or to Spetsnaz.[161] When Sweden's conservative daily paper repeated the same material and included other information identified as derived from Swedish military intelligence reports, the commander in chief requested that the government press charges against the newspaper for compromising Swedish security.[162] At no point was it suggested that the information made public was incorrect, and Swedish defense forces began exercising "coup readiness against small sabotage units" in both January and April 1986. The navy and air force also began training special defensive units against sabotage forces.[163]

In mid-December 1985, Palme made a major foreign policy address, the entire first third of which dealt with the issue of the submarine violations. The following extracts are from this portion of the address:

> Swedish territory is to be protected against incursions by all available means. Confidence in our will and capacity to protect our neutrality must be maintained. Neither fears nor hopes should be created that Sweden would abandon its neutrality policy as a result of strong, external pressure. What I said on the 8th of October, 1982, is an expression of the firmness and continuity with which Swedish neutrality policy is conducted. . . .

The duties of the Swedish armed forces also include contributing to the protection of our territory in peacetime. We are determined to repel by all available means, all those who violate our territory, our air space or our waters. We stand adamantly by our territorial integrity. We shall be masters in our own house. This is also an essential portion of the Swedish neutrality policy.

The past three years have tested the strength of this policy. At the time of the change of government in 1982, the navy was carrying out an intensive search for foreign submarines in Hårsfjärden and adjacent waters. In April 1983, the Submarine Defense Commission made public its judgement that it was Soviet submarines that had violated Swedish territory. The same day the government protested to the Soviet Union with the sharpest diplomatic note possible.

Since that time, the Commander-in-Chief has reviewed observations and indications in his quarterly reports and this has led to the conclusion that underwater activities have also been carried out by foreign powers since 1982. The difference is that, despite all our efforts, it has been impossible to identify the nation or nations involved. Thus the prerequisites necessary for diplomatic actions to be taken against a particular state have not existed. . . .

Already in October 1982, I made it clear—in a special statement—that the Swedish government has the opportunity to order the armed forces to sink a foreign submarine operating in Swedish waters. I said that anyone contemplating a violation of Swedish territory ought to include in their calculations the fact that the government will avail itself of this possibility. That statement remains valid even today. . . .

We have created respect in our region for our determination to protect Swedish territory by all possible means. . . . And I can assure you that we will continue to take rigorous action against all violations of our territory. . . . All are aware that we have new rules which make it possible that these possibilities can be resorted to quickly and that the armed forces can sink a foreign submarine operating in Swedish waters. . . .

And all are aware of the importance Swedish public opinion attaches to the hunt for submarines, and what weight — in terms of diplomatic relations — is attached to the non-violation of our territory. We have clear notice that this message has now been received in other countries. . . .

The serious violations by Soviet submarines in 1981 and 1982, along with the overflight of Gotland in the summer of 1984, have created strains in our relations with the Soviet Union.

We never hesitated to protest firmly against the Soviet incursions. We do not bend when it comes to questions of our own sovereignty. And we are of the opinion that it is best for all parties that our viewpoints are set forward in a free exchange of opinions. We shall have sufficient self-confidence to look the superpowers directly in the eye. I pointed out that at the Social Democratic Party's congress last year. . . .

In the spring, I will make an official visit to the Soviet Union at the invitation of that country's government. In Moscow I will say that we in Sweden wish to have good relations with the USSR. I will stress that these relations must be built on the basis of mutual respect for the basic rules of international law and on respect for our territorial integrity. And I am convinced that such a visit is in accord with the desire of a broad majority of the Swedish people for good and friendly relations with all our neighbors.[164]

Palme's remarks on the question of submarine violations were undoubtedly stronger and more extensive than would have been made in the absence of the protests by military officers a month before. Though Palme actually read the operative paragraphs of the IKFN regulations into his speech, these "new rules" explicitly do *not* provide that the armed forces "can sink a foreign submarine operating in Swedish waters," except inadvertently. They stipulate that the submarine should be "forced to the surface." Homing torpedoes have never been used in the ASW operations, and an explicit government order was still necessary for the use of mines.

Following the elections, Palme replaced a "strong" defense minister and a "weak" foreign minister. Only a week after the above address he abstained from participating in a security policy debate in the Parliament. In January the government also replaced an experienced Social Democratic politician who was considered strong and independent as chairman of the Parliamentary Defense Committee in the terminal stages of its work.[165] Palme's remarks quoted above were his last on the subject. He was assassinated on the evening of February 28, 1986, and his successor, Prime Minister Ingvar Carlsson, made the trip to Moscow on April 14, 1986.[166]

Soviet Press Reaction

Soviet press commentary in 1985 was somewhat more subdued. When the Swedish Parliamentary Defense Committee released a report in May 1985 that included several pages on the submarine violations, *Izvestia* carried a story about

> a new anti-submarine outburst – the stubborn wish of Swedish military and right-wing circles to whip up a hostile atmosphere against the USSR, in particular through spreading the myth about the violation of Swedish territorial waters by Soviet submarines. . . .
>
> As far as the USSR is concerned, it has repeatedly made official statements that Soviet ships have never deliberately violated Sweden's territorial integrity. The Soviet Union does not pursue any aims that could be detrimental to Sweden's political or defence interests. Moreover, the USSR wishes to develop good relations with its neighbour Sweden in the spirit of mutual respect and understanding. The maintenance of such relations also serves the interests of Sweden.[167]

There was one new theme introduced into the Soviet press in mid-1984 and continued through 1985 – the "vindictive pressure" and intimidation that Sweden was being subjected to by the United States so as to utilize Sweden for NATO interests.

> There is . . . an attempt at bringing pressure to bear on neutral Sweden in a bid to inveigle her into the ambit of the aggressive, reckless policy of the U.S. or, at least, somehow moderate the Swedes anti-militarist approach to the key problems of modern times. . . .
>
> Such efforts have no support from the general public of the North European countries, which is increasingly conscious that the Soviet Union, guiding itself as it does by the principle of equality and equal security, has never sought, nor is it seeking to change the power balance to its own advantage, and that it is in earnest in its desire to build its relations with its North-Western neighbors on the bedrock of equal rights and mutually advantageous cooperation.[168]

At the time of the new Swedish prime minister's visit to Moscow in April 1986, Soviet press commentary returned to the themes of "fabricated problems" contrived by Swedish "right wing circles," and the rhetorical question posed in May 1983 in *Izvestia*, as to who benefits by the allegations of Soviet border violations in the Swedish mass media.

1986

Two contrasting events dominated the submarine issue in 1986. The first was the visit of Prime Minister Ingvar Carlsson to Moscow in April, during which he met with both General Secretary Mikhail Gorbachev and Soviet Prime Minister Nikolai Ryzhkov. Soviet submarine violations were not on the agenda. On his return to Sweden, Carlsson said that both his hosts had expressed "unqualified respect for Sweden's neutrality policy."[169] The second event was the release on October 20 of the Defense staff's report on violations in the third quarter of 1986. Some 15 submarine incursions had allegedly taken place within these months.[170] The most senior member of the government to comment was Foreign Minister Sten Andersson, who lamely remarked that "someone or some do not show respect for our borders."[171] Sweden's two newly commissioned coastal corvettes were nevertheless in dock for a month during the height of the summer, and it was reported that the four heavy helicopters, which were the core element in the government's rapid reinforcement of Sweden's ASW capabilities following the SDC's report in April 1983, would only become fully available for use in 1989.

In October former Swedish Ambassador Sverker Åström, who was a colleague of Olof Palme's, referred to the continuing violations as "Soviet."[172] No more than two weeks later (and the very day after the release of the Defense staff report), Finland's President Koivisto returned to the position he held prior to visiting with Palme in April 1984. During a visit to Stockholm he reported that Soviet officials had assured the Finnish government that it was not their submarines that were violating Swedish waters and that they had suggested "that it would be a good thing if the Swedes used effective fire against the intruders, as that would show that the Soviet Union was speaking truthfully."[173]

At the end of the month, *Pravda* printed an interview with Prime Minister Carlsson in which he stated that "Swedish-Soviet relations have recently developed in a positive direction. But it is worth pointing out that I consider a real improvement in a number of areas as necessary. That must occur on the basis of respect for national sovereignty and the inviolability of borders."[174]

In November the Defense staff reported that two additional submarine violations, one in 1980 and one in 1982, had been absolutely identified as having been made by Warsaw Pact submarines.[175] (In addition to the U-137 and the Hårsfjärden identifications which involved four vessels, this made four certain identifications.) The head of the Swedish navy reported that Sweden's ASW capabilities still did not serve to deter against violation by foreign submarines, and the former head of the Swedish navy's submarine incidents analyses group published a scathing commentary on the state of Swedish ASW capabilities and government policies.[176]

4

An Analysis of the Incursions

Three main subjects will be discussed in the analysis: the Swedish government's response to the submarine violations, the apparent attitudes of the USSR, and the motives behind the Soviet submarine operations.

Sweden's Response

The Swedish governments that have been in office while these violations have occurred have indicated that the credibility of Sweden's neutrality policy depended above all else on the demonstration of both Sweden's will and its ability to protect the country's territorial integrity. Everyone has agreed that the submarine violations are a test of both that will and capability. In the words of Prime Minister Palme, the submarine intrusion incidents went "to the heart of our neutrality policy." Without exception, Swedish spokesmen, civilian as well as military and irrespective of political affiliation, have emphasized after every event that the Swedish attempts to force the submarines to the surface or to leave Swedish waters emphatically demonstrated that will. It would seem, however, that the conclusions that the USSR has drawn after more than seven years of these operations are more likely to be exactly the opposite.

The dilemma facing the Swedish government involved one of the most difficult choices for any nation's national security policy: to reject a strategic warning that is politically uncomfortable, or to opt for appeasement. Given the unwillingness of nonsocialist and socialist governments alike to sink a submarine, the Swedish government found itself at a loss to know what to do about the territorial violations. Purchase of new equipment would have no impact for perhaps four or five years and orders to force submarines to the surface were clearly ineffective given the resources available and the way in which they were applied. One could even question the degree to which new equipment would alter the picture as long as operational orders remained the same. Despite his public threats on three occasions between the spring of 1983 and December 1985 regarding the possibility of sinking a submarine, Palme was firmly resolved not to do so. Many government officials believed that the incidents would end after each major event, and the longer they continued, the more the cessation was expected. Some expected the incursions to end after the 1980 Utö/Huvudskär events, more after the U-137 stranding and the Swedish protest, still more after the Hårsfjärden episode, the SDC report and the Swedish protest note, Palme's meeting with Gromyko, and the initiation of the CDE. Palme apparently had hoped that they would end after he took office. But in each case the events continued.[1]

The degree of confusion shown by the Swedish government is demonstrated by the fact that as late as May 1984 Palme said that Sweden did not know if its message had yet reached the Soviet Politburo. In 1980 and 1981, the Swedish government tended to believe that submarine operations were being carried out under the authorization of Soviet military officials without the knowledge of the senior Soviet political leadership. This notion became less tenable as the operations continued even after repeated Swedish government protests. By December 1985 Palme could say that the Swedish message had been received, but he had

certainly not obtained the "signal" and the "binding assurances" that he had requested in May 1983 to indicate that
the incursions would stop.

The questions for Sweden were the following ones:

- Were the submarine violations continuing?
- If so, why couldn't the Swedish navy force one to the
  surface?
- If the submarine incursions were continuing, what
  nation was responsible for them?
- If they were Soviet submarines, what should Sweden's behavior be vis-à-vis the USSR?

It is clear that the submarine violations did continue, despite the ambiguous phrasing used now and then by the
prime minister and the foreign minister and the government's tendency to make believe that it were not so. The
question of capabilities and operational performance has
several answers. In the 1970s, Swedish politicians counted
on U.S.-Soviet détente to permit the Swedish navy to phase
out its ASW mission while defense priorities emphasized a
strong invasion defense, including air defense. The only
problem was an excessively narrow definition of "invasion
defense," which did not seem to include ASW capabilities.
Countering the ability of small elite units to come ashore
covertly and destroy ships, coastal defense guns, radars,
and command facilities is also a part of invasion defense,
perhaps even a quintessential part.

As to performance during the actual ASW operations,
this can perhaps best be summed up in two comments, the
first made by a senior naval officer: "It isn't enough that we
are half blind"—referring to the lack of sensors—"but we
also have one or two arms behind our back."[2] The second
assessed the times in which the navy was certain of its
contacts with a submarine in internal waters: "The right
weapon didn't exist. Or it wasn't at the right place. Or one
couldn't use it."[3] It is difficult for an outside observer to
determine to what degree naval performance has been inad-

equate and to what degree the standing order to force a submarine to the surface — ostensibly undamaged — is impossible.[4] The official reports of the two major ASW operations, Hårsfjärden in October 1982 and Karlskrona in March 1984, nevertheless criticize excessive problems in command and operations. The conclusion may be that the overall result has been a combination of three major contributing elements: inadequate equipment and capabilities, poor performance and snafus, and the political restriction on a military response. These undoubtedly all played a part, possibly interacting to different degrees during different events.

It would have been impossible for the government to maintain the remainder of its policies without the pretense surrounding the question of identifying the nationality of the intruding submarines. When Anders Thunborg left office as defense minister in September 1985, he made it clear that the Defense Ministry had "a definite understanding" as to which nation was responsible for the submarine incursions. Senior military officers said the same, and a *Dagens Nyheter* editorial in March 1986 indicated that there was "considerable unity" that "the country was exposed to Soviet submarine activities. . . ."[5] Nevertheless, the requirements of the government's public posture required tortuous explanations. The following comments by the newly appointed foreign minister in November 1985 are an example.

> Q: If the Soviet Union indicates so clearly that it wants to have good relations with Sweden, then it certainly will not send any submarines into Swedish waters in the future?
>
> A: No; that is the assumption I am working on.
>
> Q: So the five definite submarine incursions that the C-in-C identified in his most recent quarterly report do not come from the Warsaw Pact?
>
> A: One can't make such an assumption. The C-in-C could not determine their nationality and as a result Sweden cannot react diplomatically.
>
>   One cannot carry out a foreign policy that is

> based on suspicion. If one begins to construct one's
> foreign policy of distrust and speculations, then
> that will be an extremely risky policy. The national-
> ity of the submarines could not be determined and a
> foreign policy must be based on facts.[6]

Sweden was hardly guilty of abstract distrust and random speculation, however. The inability to establish a submarine's nationality operationally meant at the most the inability to decide whether the recording of a Whisky submarine's motor was of a Soviet or Polish submarine. That determination was not the opposite of "a fact." The failure to make a diplomatic response gave the appearance that nothing had occurred. The suggestion in a 1984 report by the Parliamentary Defense Committee and in a January 1986 submission by the new defense minister that submarine violations after 1982 were "similar" to those for which the USSR had been identified as responsible in Hårsfjärden in 1982 was meaningful only to the initiated, particularly as the comments were followed by paragraphs restating the government's inability to identify the intruders after 1982.[7] The significance of Palme's suggestion in a December 1985 radio interview that the submarine incursions were "a part of the modern acquisition of knowledge," which the USSR and the United States carried out near each other's coasts with the aid of submarines, was the implied recognition that the submarines in Swedish internal waters were Soviet.[8]

There was also the question of the wisdom of dissembling. A Finnish commentator asked what the Swedish government would do even if the USSR openly admitted responsibility for the continuing incursions. "It is good that they lie," he stated. The situation would of course be equally undesirable for the Finns if Sweden could prove Soviet responsibility.[9] One Finnish commentary referred to the Swedish reaction as "slightly hysterical." In this view the reality of Soviet behavior and of Soviet-Swedish relations was not so much what actually took place, but what was said. Another Finnish commentary – from the editor of Finland's Swedish-language daily newspaper and a former Finnish presidential candidate – was to the effect that the Swedes should not get excited; if they got angry at the USSR, it would only make problems for Finland. The events are just "temporary," and the Swedes should just relax and accept them.[10] The most sophisticated inversion of causality, in commentary both in Sweden and in Finland, was that "the USSR doubts Swedish neutrality." This argument explaining why the USSR was responsible for the submarine incursions implied that it was Sweden's fault; Sweden is suspect, it favors the West, it has brought the situation on itself.[11] The Soviet submarine operations were therefore "defensive." Nevertheless, there was a strong desire to claim that irrespective of whatever had (or had not) taken place, the events had not changed anything. "The Nordic situation was still the same."[12] Another Finnish source phrased this in a slightly modified way, suggesting that the activities were "a Soviet way of getting Sweden to emphasize its neutrality more frequently and clearly. The USSR has a need to obtain affirming declarations of that kind constantly. They want to hear repeatedly that Swedish neutrality has not altered."[13] The logic that finds submarine incursions of the type that took place as a means of provoking a Swedish statement of neutrality is at the least tortuous.

In the background there were also always a substantial number of bizarre theories: the navigation of the U-137 was either accidental – or alcoholic; NATO submarines were responsible; the bottom markings had been made by Swedish submarines; a retired British admiral suggested that the Swedes were suffering from "periscope sickness"; there were no submarines at all. As late as October 1985, a major editorial writer for *Dagens Nyheter* could write that "two grandiose theories stand opposed in the submarine debate. One is the Submarine Defense Commission's. The other . . . [that] The Swedish military has succeeded in deceiving an entire nation."[14] In 1983, a former Danish Social Democratic

minister wrote in the Danish Social Democratic party newspaper, that "there aren't any Soviet submarines in Swedish waters and there never have been any; it is all
a pure invention to get more money for the military
services."[15]

The most difficult question was of course what policy
should Sweden follow in response to the submarine violations. Swedish policy clearly was unable to face realities
and their unpleasant, complicating implications. Late in
the fall of 1982, Defense Minister Thunborg addressed an
annual Swedish defense policy convocation. The title of his
speech was "Our Neutrality is Respected by the World
Around Us."[16] By that time the submarine commission had
been empanelled, and Thunborg knew that the statement
was most definitely not true, at least if his speech was
meant to refer to the USSR. In 1986 he still maintained
that "Our determined will to protect our territory has been
met by respect in our region."[17] We have already noted Foreign Minister Bodström's remarks in April 1985, immediately after the Karlskrona events, to the effect that the
Soviet Union's only interests were good relations with Sweden. Bodström had also repeated Gromyko's claim that the
USSR had not violated Swedish territory since the 1981
submarine stranding, without noting the Swedish government's own official opinion to the contrary. Palme himself
attributed to Gromyko the statements that he had hoped
the Soviet foreign minister would make.

This pattern was also reflected in the degree to which
the domestic political debate dealt with what was said rather than what was done. The most important problem often
seemed to be obtaining consensus on what to say, rather
than on stopping the incursions themselves.[18] Some months
before Prime Minister Palme's anticipated visit to the
USSR, a *Dagens Nyheter* editorial noted that "the reluc-
tance shown in the radio interviews [by opposition spokes-
men] to draw conclusions about the implications of the submarine incursions following Hårsfjärden was certainly
striking – and surely wise."[19]

One can generalize about these responses to some degree by pointing out that they are similar to important elements of Sweden's approach to major international political and arms control problems, which is to describe the world as Sweden wants it to be rather than as it is: with continued repetition, those whose behavior one wants to change will inevitably be constrained – if not perhaps convinced – to act accordingly. It is not so much "Speak Truth to Power," but "Speak Morality to Power" – the hope of utilizing the potential leverage of morality and the norms of international legal restrictions to obtain a change in the behavior of some nation. There may be much to commend the practice in certain contexts, but it can only produce an immediate dissonance with reality.

In the case of the submarines, moreover, Sweden was on its own territory and was not without power. The government did not want to use that power in the one way that would have put a more rapid end to the incursions – to damage severely or to sink an intruding submarine. In one of the extremely rare instances in which there was any public explanation of the reasoning behind this decision, "a leading Social Democrat" explained that

> Dozens of dead Soviet soldiers as a result of a Swedish act of war in peacetime would be a nightmare. Sweden would be forced to consultations and to respond to Soviet demands for apologies, damages, and assurances that attacks on ships suffering navigation failure and accidents and with young fathers on board would not be repeated.[20]

If the government that owned the submarine were concerned for the safety of its naval personnel, it would be very simple to keep the submarine in international waters. That is its responsibility. These considerations are not the responsibility of the prime minister of a state determined to maintain its territorial integrity "with all available means" and determined to demonstrate that it "has both the will and the capability to carry out its declared policy also in the case of war and in difficult situations."[21]

In one week of September 1983, submarine activity in five different locations along the Swedish coast was reported, and 20 to 40 incidents were estimated to have taken place in the summer of 1983 alone.[22] Nevertheless, Swedish military authorities and the government have maintained that it has not been possible to identify the nationality of any of the intruding submarines since the fall of 1982. This claim — even if technically justified — along with the skepticism expressed at times by senior Swedish political authorities that there may have been no further intrusions after 1982 was presumably intended to serve as a diplomatic device that would facilitate the end of the operations by the USSR. Under this rationale, if the USSR were not identified openly as the source of the operations, it would be easier for the Soviet leadership to terminate them. Perhaps this would be so if there were any apparent need for diplomatic ingenuity to devise "a way out" to end the operations. But there was no such need, and there was still no evidence in 1986 that the USSR showed any interest in stopping the incursions.

There is a profound and basic political risk in the policy Sweden chose to follow. Making believe that one does not see things as they are can be extremely dangerous. A nation's political health is not strengthened when the government dissembles. Partial truths, if continuously indulged, are more likely to lead to an inability to see things as they are. This is far more dangerous political "rot" than the one Palme found so distressing — criticism from his domestic political opposition. At the same time, the prime minister showed little hesitation in greatly exaggerating his attacks on the domestic political opposition. When the nonsocialist parties in Parliament moved a vote of no confidence against the foreign minister after his remarks in February 1985, Palme termed them a threat to Sweden's neutrality policy and declared that a nonsocialist government "would constitute a serious danger for Sweden's peace." Palme was essentially successful in his efforts to transform criticism of his policies into criticism of his opponents. The political risk of his policies was indicated in the parliamentary foreign policy debate in the spring of 1984 when Palme questioned the privilege of an open foreign policy debate where the criticism "is unjustified, and simultaneously deals with vital security interests as basic elements of Swedish foreign policy."[23] In a TV interview the same year, Palme added that it was not compatible with Swedish neutrality policy to scrutinize critically the purposes of the Soviet leadership if the analyses supported the "devil's images" that are found in the United States.

The unwillingness to face unpleasant realities was demonstrated in lesser ways as well. For several years in the early 1980s, a faction within the ruling Social Democratic Party was prepared to accept the occasional joking suggestion that all the activity in the archipelago was contrived by the military services to obtain budget increases. Defense Minister Thunborg had to argue before the 1984 party congress that if Sweden no longer provided the military means to prevent violations of its borders, its plan to remain neutral in a future war would lose its credibility, and that "the hawks wouldn't become more peaceful if one clipped the wings of the doves."[24] Two reallocations and only a single increase in military expenditure were decided on as a direct consequence of the submarine incursion events over a period of three years:

- 150 million crowns were reallocated after the Utö/ Huvudskär incidents in 1980;
- 200 million crowns were reallocated after the U-137 stranding in 1981;
- 250 million crowns were supplied as additional expenditure after the submarine commission report on Hårsfjärden in 1983.

These 600 million crowns — around $70 million in 1983–1984 exchange rates — were, however, to be divided over five years (about $14 million per year) for the procurement of ships, helicopters, sonar equipment, and for operating costs. In 1983 it was estimated that 1.2 billion crowns, or just double the above sum, would be earmarked for these purposes for the 10 years between 1982 and 1992.[25] Of 950 million crowns in funds earmarked for ASW between 1980 and 1990, 450 million were reallocated within the navy and 300 million were reallocated from the other military services.[26] Only the 250 million crowns, or roughly $30 million, represented new expenditure. Though the new ASW systems that could be procured with these sums appeared impressive against the background of the nearly total absence that preceded them, (see table 6) the increment of approximately 1 percent was small in view of the five years of submarine activity and a total Swedish defense expenditure of 20 billion crowns (or $2.33 billion) in FY 1983–1984. Substantial increases in defense expenditures were expected in 1986, although the new defense minister expressed a preference for emphasis to be put on aircraft and air defense rather than on ASW.[27]

Western commentators have often questioned why the Soviet Union should have taken the risks inherent in the submarine incursion program. The political costs of disclosure would be substantial: embarrassment in the international political arena and a setback to proposals for a Nordic Nuclear-Free Zone, which the USSR ostensibly desires. If a submarine had actually been sunk or severely damaged and forced to the surface deep inside a restricted Swedish military zone, there would perhaps have been political costs to the USSR. But the Swedish government avoided such action, and there were few if any costs.

It was particularly unlikely that there would be costly repercussions of long duration in Sweden, where it mattered the most. The reason for that, which has not been well understood in the West, is precisely Sweden's neutrality policy and, above all, its interpretation under the Social Democratic government that held office at the time. (Social Democratic governments have held office, alone or in coalition, for the entire post-World War II period except for 1976 to 1982.) What could the Swedish government do, aside from making some small increments to its defense expenditures? First, Sweden's own neutrality policy forbade any overt moves toward a closer orientation to NATO. In practice, this policy even made it difficult for the government to explain quietly and simply that the USSR was being hostile and was openly displaying itself as a potential enemy, even though that may have been the meaning of the conclusions of the Submarine Defense Commission. The difficulty was also reflected in the somewhat perverse formulation of some Swedish military analysts that explained the Soviet activities as being no more than the "natural" accompaniment to planning at the Soviet General Staff level.

Second, Sweden saw no desirable outcome in a spiraling exacerbation of tension and hostility with the USSR. Experience indicated that the Soviet government would not draw back, despite its responsibility for the problems. The result of this calculus was that Sweden would be forced – to maintain the "balance" that had come to accompany Sweden's neutrality policy – to return to a "back-to-normal" policy with the USSR six months after each major incident.

That is exactly what happened, and somewhat sooner. The Swedish government was already involved in a concerted back-to-normal effort while the major submarine incursion was taking place in Karlskrona in March 1984. It formally approved the exchange of ministerial level visits with the USSR in that period. More often than not it was the Swedish ministers who traveled to the USSR. Having sent his message to the Soviet leadership with its three demands, Palme could hardly announce that these had been crudely rejected by the USSR, which continued its submarine violations. And so, of course, he said nothing. The Soviets preempted the entire process, moreover, by attacking Swedish neutrality as too pro-Western during 1982 and 1983; this was, of course, the gist of Gromyko's message in January 1984.

The report of the submarine commission described the

submarine incursions as being of a "military operational character." The government—the prime minister, defense minister, and foreign minister—all spoke, however, in numerous public statements in more abstract terms of the increased importance of the general Nordic/Scandinavian area in the USSR-U.S. strategic nuclear competition and sometimes more specifically and more accurately of the disposition of the Soviet Northern Fleet on the Kola Peninsula. In an interview in *Newsweek* in October 1983, Prime Minister Palme was asked why he thought the Soviets had been making these incursions. He replied that it was "a sign that the Baltic area has become strategically more important in recent years. The buildup of the Kola Peninsula and the buildup of NATO forces in the area have contributed to this increased interest."[28] Palme added that "it is certainly not a preparation for war. It is a kind of espionage," a judgment that contradicted the conclusions of the submarine commission's report. In April 1984, Sweden's foreign minister expressed a position even more generalized than Palme's: "The frozen relations between the superpowers had caused the problems for Sweden by increasing international tension." Sweden and the submarine incursions were thus in some way linked to this larger and more general problem. This sort of explanation had two effects: it qualified the apparent belligerence of the USSR and presented the United States as at least a partial contributor to the problem. It also deflected the issue away from Sweden per se. Neither the commission nor the government ever attempted to explain why Sweden in particular was getting this type of military attention from the USSR and why in these precise years.

Early in 1985 there appeared a somewhat modified interpretation of the course of the submarine incursions over the years. The experience gained from the events during 1980–1985, particularly as regards various sensor recordings, led to a reappraisal of evidence that had been discounted between 1970 and 1980 on the assumption that the observations came from areas that were too shallow to permit submarine operations. These newer conclusions were presumed to some degree by the SDC, but they were only put forward publicly in 1985.[29] The revised sequence of the history of intrusions by foreign submarines now appeared to be as follows:

- Even in the 1950s and 1960s conventional-sized submarines penetrated deep into Swedish internal waters, as well as into the territorial sea.
- Soviet submarines must have had substantial operating experience deep inside Swedish internal waters long before they began the more provocative maneuvers of 1980 and later. They had to know their general way about in the channels of the archipelago and the harbor basin exits to feel confident of their ability to escape in the face of concerted ASW operations should these take place.
- Some time after the mid-1970s, operations using the midget submarines began, at first intermittently, in a technical and tactical testing phase.
- From around 1977–1978, the midget submarines appeared in operational units in coordinated, large-scale incursions.

The first of these operations was, however, apparently not detected by Swedish naval units until the spring and fall of 1980.

There was one hypothetical consequence of this new interpretation. Soviet officials may possibly have assumed that the Swedish government knew of the earlier incursions and preferred to keep silent about them. The Swedish effort after 1980 to stop the incursions and direct public attention to them at least in part would then have appeared as a change – as if the USSR were now being deprived of something that had previously been permitted. The plausibility of this speculation depends in part on the judgment of Soviet submarine officers as to whether they had been detected or not on earlier occasions. Swedish naval vessels had reacted at least in some cases when submarines were detected in earlier years, and only Soviet officials knew how many submarines had been missed. What is more significant is that the earlier one presumes the submarine operations to have entered their second phase involving midget submarines, the earlier in the "decade of détente" they began.

Soviet Actions

The Soviet Union carried out submarine activities in Swedish waters during the tenure of at least four party secretaries: Brezhnev, Andropov, Chernenko, and Gorbachev. Sweden and Norway appear to be the only location in Western Europe in which the USSR carries out this sort of activity on any extended scale. At its peak, between 40 and 60 violations a year were recorded, an average of 1 per week. Because ice conditions in the archipelago restricted operations for several months of the year, the frequency must have been even higher at other times.

The evidence that the oldest class of Whisky submarines carry nuclear torpedoes in the Baltic, in peacetime, and even in such operations as these also raised important questions about the Soviet's expectations about the nature of warfare at sea and about their own intentions as to the possible early initiation of tactical nuclear warfare at sea. The activities began before 1980, that is, in the period before U.S.-USSR and East-West détente ran into serious difficulties. The submarine incursions were carried out with impunity, particularly in internal waters. They also were continued openly after official notes of protest from the Swedish government. The USSR did not even hesitate to carry out these operations in the country that was host to the CDE while the conference was taking place. During their operations the submarines even traveled partially exposed for brief periods, either for tactical reasons or because forced to by navigational conditions.

It would appear that the intrusions were substantially increased after the stranding of the U-137 submarine and the subsequent Swedish protest, as if to demonstrate to Sweden that the Soviet Union would continue to act as it pleased. The apparent increase may be in part a consequence of Sweden's greater alertness after 1981 and the uncertainty regarding the actual frequency of the earlier incursions. It is clear, nevertheless, that the operations successively penetrated deeper inshore, because bottom tracks were found where they had not previously been.

The Soviet government has not hesitated to lie to the Swedish government, even when the Swedish government knew with absolute certainty that the USSR was lying. Soviet government representatives did this at the highest political level: in meetings between Soviet Foreign Minister Gromyko and Sweden's Prime Minister Palme and in messages from General Secretary Andropov via Finnish President Koivisto. Submarine operations were carried out on the day that the Swedish government's investigative committee released its report and two weeks after Ambassador Ferm transmitted Prime Minister Palme's message that he wanted a signal from the USSR that the operations would end. In addition, the USSR termed the Swedish protest note and the commission's report "an unfriendly act." The Soviet government then watched Swedish officials maintain for four years that they could not identify the nationality of the intruding submarines. The one party that was not fooled was the USSR.

For a time, the operations raised important questions about military-political decision making in the USSR and the operational prerogatives of the Soviet military leadership in peacetime. These questions concerned areas of responsibility, oversight, and approval that are difficult to resolve externally. In the period between the stranding of the U-137 submarine in Karlskrona in October 1981 and the events at Hårsfjärden in October 1982, there was substantial discussion in Swedish government circles as to whether the submarine operations were being carried out by the

Soviet military without the knowledge of the senior Soviet political leadership. This would seem unlikely. There are at least three senior individuals in the USSR who can be presumed to know of all operations carried out by Soviet forces that have any security or defense implications: the minister of defense, the chief of the General Staff, and the Communist Party's general secretary. Each of these individuals would be informed through subordinates on their staffs, raising the number of informed individuals at the command and oversight levels. Of these three, the defense minister and, of course, the general secretary were both in the Politburo. During the years in question, Marshal Dmitrij Ustinov was the minister of defense. He was considered a member of the most senior Soviet political hierarchy, not a representative of the military services.

The Swedish submarine commission report released in April 1983 following the Hårsfjärden events took the position that the submarine operations were carried out with the knowledge of the Soviet political leadership. The Swedish government nevertheless still distanced itself from this judgment, and its protest note to the USSR requested that the Soviet government order the Soviet navy to stop the incursions. At a press conference at the time of the commission's report, Palme was asked what position he held on the question. He pointed out that the commission believed that the Soviet political leadership was informed of and must have approved the operations, but that there were experts who disagreed; he did not want to express a definite opinion on the subject. He did think, however, "that it is unlikely that the political leadership could avoid having knowledge about these things."[30] The only direct evidence on the question appeared in the book published in early 1985 by Arkady Shevchenko, a senior member of the Soviet foreign ministry who had defected to the United States in 1978. In *Breaking with Moscow*, Shevchenko claims that the Politburo approved plans for submarine operations in Norwegian and Swedish waters at a meeting in 1970. Ironically, Shevchenko also claims that the Politburo took this decision just as or after Palme visited Moscow in 1970 during his tenure as prime minister in an earlier Social Democratic government and was given Soviet assurances that the USSR wanted to broaden cooperation with Sweden.

Soviet public response to the events seemed to take place on three levels, aside from the continuation of the operations themselves. The first was the official diplomatic rejection of the Swedish notes. The second was the public press comment, some for publication within the USSR and some for external publication, which included a multitude of themes denying all Soviet responsibility for the events. Soviet press commentaries maintained that the Swedish reports were fabrications and provocations, Swedish or Norwegian fantasies, plants of NATO or of the U.S. Department of Defense, or the result of a conspiracy of Swedish right-wing and military quarters designed to obtain larger expenditures for the Swedish military. The Swedish government's official protest note after Hårsfjärden was never reported in the domestic Soviet press. It was impossible for the USSR to be responsible, because no Soviet submarines approach within 30 km of the Swedish coast; the U-137 stranding was a navigational error.

The third response was an intermediate level made up of the comments by senior Soviet government spokesmen. Such comments often repeated portions of the official Soviet notes of rejection, but for the most part they abstained from the ridicule and invective of the Soviet press commentaries. Instead, they all emphasized two themes. The first stressed that the USSR desires good relations with Sweden; it is the fault of Sweden for impeding these relations by all this talk about submarines. The second theme posed the rhetorical question: "Who benefits by the cooling in our [USSR-Swedish] relations? The Soviet Union stands for peace and good neighborly relations based on mutual respect." The implied answer was NATO, the United States, and the Pentagon – those who favor war and armaments. Obviously, then, the Swedish complaints only produce undesirable effects and therefore should be stopped.[31] Sweden found itself manipulated into replying to a fictitious level of parlance in which guilt and responsibility are inverted.

As early as April 1981, exactly halfway between the Utö-Huvudskär and Hårsfjärden incidents, a Soviet government spokesman published an article in the Swedish daily press under the title "Good Neighborly Relations: Sweden-Soviet Union."[32] In September 1983, Vadim Zagladin attended a conference on "Common Security" in Sweden. He explained that the Swedish government had declared on numerous occasions that it wanted to develop ties with the USSR, but that the Swedish commander in chief was not enthusiastic about good relations between the two states. Zagladin also added that "I have spoken with our highest military chiefs and they have explained to me that there are no instructions concerning such activities [submarine intrusions] in Swedish waters."[33] It was also Zagladin who criticized Swedish neutrality policy as being too pro-Western during 1982 and 1983. In October 1983, Soviet General Viktor Tatarnikov, identified as a member of the Soviet General Staff, warned that the United States was behind the allegations of submarine incursions in Swedish waters and that these were an attempt to "trap" Sweden: "The U.S. sought to develop a political climate in which it would be necessary for Sweden to accept the placement of U.S. naval contingents in Swedish waters in order to protect Sweden against Soviet submarines."[34] If Swedish naval sources repeated such naive and false claims alleging that the bottom depression marks at Hårsfjärden matched the U-137 keel dimensions taken at the time of its stranding, then this would lead to the situation that the U.S. desired—Sweden would ask for U.S. naval assistance.

In the spring of 1984, Alexander Bovin, *Izvestia*'s senior political columnist, published his critique in the Swedish press entitled "Who Benefits By This Constant Cooling?" of Swedish-USSR relations. In the fall of 1984, Zagladin went on the attack again, charging that there were shortcomings in the Swedish neutrality policy; Sweden should practice "a more active peace policy"; efforts to provide a strong Swedish defense were misguided; Sweden's one-sided dependence on the United States and NATO was increasing; and Swedish threat perceptions assumed an attack only from the east. He also thought that it was "no accident" that a submarine incident "cropped up every time a Swedish parliamentary or ministerial visit to the USSR was due."[35] These criticisms were repeated in an unusual Soviet book published in English late in 1984. Written by Lev Voronkov, the book was called *Non-Nuclear Status to Northern Europe*. It stressed three main points about Sweden. First, it charged that Swedish neutrality policy was too Western, American, and NATO oriented – a repetition of Zagladin's charges and the theme of a Soviet press campaign in 1982. Second, it suggested that Sweden should carry out "a more active neutrality and peace oriented policy," the suggestion that Zagladin and Georgi Arbatov had also made on previous occasions. Finally, it urged Sweden to work harder to achieve a Nordic Nuclear-Free Zone, a repetition of Gromyko's request and a theme that had also been part of the press campaign in 1982. Voronkov also suggested that Sweden should reduce its defense spending.[36] Prior to the expected visit to Prime Minister Palme to the USSR in 1986, a Soviet official, writing in the Swedish press under a pseudonym, noted that "As expected, it quickly became obvious what an untenable idea it was to apply 'sanctions' against the USSR by curtailing political and other contacts," as if it were only the USSR that was interested in such contacts.[37]

There are several strong reasons to doubt that the USSR considers a Nordic Nuclear-Free Zone a real possibility. To begin with, Sweden and Finland already are nuclear free in both war and peace. As for Norway and Denmark, they are also nuclear free in peacetime, as required by their foreign and defense policies, and it is unlikely that they could enter into an agreement that set any wartime restrictions as long as they remain members of NATO. In discussing the concept of a Nordic Nuclear-Free Zone, Norwegian spokesmen have pointed out that it is only meaningful in peacetime. Meanwhile, Sweden has consistently stated that such a zone would require inclusion not only of the Baltic but also constraints on nuclear weapons in adjacent territory as well as weapons intended for use in the zone.[38] The more or less consistent Swedish interpretations range from the one by Thunborg in 1975 to Palme's Passikivi Foundation address in June 1983. This formulation was intended to apply to Soviet territory and weapons, and, because the phrasing is not exact, it runs the risk of including the Soviet Northern Fleet as well as Soviet medium-range aviation. Unquestionably, however, the sizable disposition of Soviet nuclear weapons in its Baltic Fleet and on its adjacent territory comes into question. These might include several hundred warheads in the Baltic Fleet alone.[39] In addition, 60 to 65 percent of all USSR ship repair facilities and 70 percent of its submarine repair facilities are in Baltic naval bases. In time of war, Soviet ships armed with nuclear weapons would have to be brought into the Baltic for repair at such facilities.

Senior Soviet spokesmen have at times replied that the USSR would be willing to consider constraints imposed by a Nordic nuclear-free zone on Soviet territory in the course of negotiating a treaty. The first indications of what this might mean in terms of Soviet negotiating demands appeared, however, only in Voronkov's book in 1984. Voronkov argued that the Central European states that bordered on the Baltic were just as concerned about such a zone as were Scandinavian states—that is, Poland and the GDR, aside from the USSR—and that the U.S. decision to place theater nuclear missiles in West Germany, a state bordering on the Baltic, was also a relevant consideration. Soviet land-based missiles in East Germany were not mentioned. In addition, Voronkov was negative about the Swedish demand that nuclear weapons in the area adjacent to the nuclear-free zone should also be withdrawn: "Any Soviet consideration of such a demand would depend on the reduction of the possibilities of nuclear attack on the USSR from areas that are adjacent to Northern Europe."

Earlier Soviet references of the same sort usually have been interpreted to mean U.S. or NATO weapons in the

North Atlantic, but they conceivably could mean U.S. weapons in West Germany or the British nuclear forces as well. To include the North Atlantic without mentioning the Soviet Northern Fleet is impossible and to assume reductions in the nuclear components of the Soviet Northern Fleet in the context of a Nordic nuclear-free zone is inconceivable. Voronkov has also been quoted as saying that nuclear weapons in the Baltic are "a part of the military balance in Europe, and should not in the first instance be seen in a Nordic perspective."[40] A Soviet spokesman, commenting on a Nordic nuclear-free zone again in 1986, referred to West German territory, and such references are perhaps the strongest reason for doubting that the USSR seeks or expects the negotiation of such a zone in the foreseeable future. As long as the USSR considers that this zone would require obligations only of the Nordic countries but no constraints on Soviet nuclear forces in the Baltic, or that, in exchange for constraints on Soviet forces, there would be constraints on the United States and NATO in the northern Atlantic or West Germany, a Nordic nuclear-free zone is out of the question.

Significantly, no important Soviet spokesmen and few of the more irresponsible Soviet press commentaries suggested that NATO or U.S. submarines were responsible for the intrusions into Swedish waters. The question was put directly to Admiral Nikolay Amelko, deputy chief of the Soviet General Staff, in May 1984: If the Soviet government denials of responsibility are correct and if the Swedish government's findings that submarines are entering Swedish water are also correct, whose submarines might they be? Admiral Amelko replied only that no Soviet submarines have been nearer than 30 km to the Swedish coast, and he doubted that any submarines were there.[41] The implications then are clear: if the USSR knew that its own submarines were not in Swedish waters, yet the Swedish military authorities and government were reporting continuous submarine incursions, that would mean NATO or U.S. submarines were operating deep inside neutral Swedish waters directly across the Baltic from the Soviet coast and at the entrance to Sweden's major naval bases. If that were indeed the case, it is difficult to imagine anything other than a strong Soviet reaction. Or imagine that the USSR had ceased its activities after Hårsfjärden and the Swedish commission's report identifying the Soviet Union as responsible for the submarine violations and then found that Western submarine incursions took place while Palme's government kept quiet. Soviet protests certainly would have been great.[42]

The Motives Behind the Soviet Submarine Operations

Norway

As the Norwegian government commission that investigated the events of May 1983 in Hardangerfjord wrote,

> Concerning possible motives for violating Norwegian territorial waters, the Select Committee can only point to traditional military needs. Thus, it is generally assumed that a foreign power, i.a., is interested in getting to know Norwegian waters and the special conditions pertaining to Norwegian territory, including the possibilities for utilizing Norwegian coastal waters, harbours and land areas.
>
> The Select Committee also points to the possibility that a submarine incident in one location might be a diversion to ensure a safe execution of operations elsewhere.[43]

The four fjord areas that have seen the largest number of incursions all permit easy access from the open sea and all lead deep into the country. There have been conflicting statements in the press as to whether the majority of the Norwegian incursions are relatively close to the major Norwegian naval bases, or whether they are particularly near to military installations. The four major Norwegian naval bases are located at Olavsvern (Tromsö), Ramsund (Harstad), Haakonsvarn (Bergen), and Karl Johans Vern (Horten). At the time of the Hardangerfjord events, naval elements of NATO's Supreme Allied Commander Atlantic (SACLANT) were visiting Bergen, relatively close to Hardangerfjord. Some of the submarine events have also been close to Andöy Island, which contains major military facilities: Orion P-3 aircraft and, according to recent disclosures in Norway, the land terminus of ASW detection facilities.[44] It has been pointed out as well that some of the areas – for example, the Tysfjord-Ofotfjord complex leading to Narvik – would be vulnerable to mine-laying by submarines.[45] In the Norwegian situation, it has been impossible for domestic skeptics to suggest that the submarines belonged to a NATO state. J. J. Holst, now Norwegian defense secretary, has commented that it is consistent with Soviet military dispositions in Europe in general to assume that the USSR plans on a forward defense in case of any conflict in Europe, that is, to do its fighting outside Soviet borders and on the territory of potential opponents.[46] In several articles Holst has listed some of the military benefits for Soviet submarines operating in Norwegian waters: an increase in the possibilities for operations against NATO vessels; a place to hide from attack; and the facilitation of an attack on Norwegian territory to land commando groups and to attack land and naval bases.[47] Holst also refers to "political pressure" as an additional benefit of submarine violations, but provides no details or just how or for what purpose such pressure might operate.

Sweden

There has been a large and bewildering array of suggestions as to the cause of the Soviet submarine operations in Swedish waters. Some explanations are basically political, others military. Some assume that the operations have been carried out in a purposefully open manner – while others assume that a degree of covertness was at least attempted. Many of these suggestions are mutually contradictory, either entirely or in part. For example, if the basic Soviet intention was the application of political pressure, it is less meaningful to speak simultaneously of "political costs." If the purposes were military and the operations were continued despite disclosure, Sweden, as well as others that could be affected, were supplied with strategic warning. The continuation of the operations surely alerted military authorities in the United States and NATO. There is also the theoretical possibility that the entire operation is a feint intended to mislead Sweden and other nations about the most likely manner of Soviet military operations in the Nordic area in wartime, but this seems unlikely due to their magnitude and persistence.

Three major questions should be kept in mind against which the various suggestions should be tested as they are reviewed:

- Why was Sweden, of all countries, the target of this particular form and degree of attention?
- Why were the violations so blatant, and why were they repeated once disclosed? For the three years of peak activity – 1982 to 1984 – when incursions ran at an annual rate of 40 to 60, it meant an average of one incursion per week. In one week in the middle of September 1983 suspected submarine incursions took place at five different points along the Swedish coast, spanning virtually half the country's coastline.
- Why did these activities take place particularly in these years?

Purposeful Provocation Theories

Military

There are two suggestions of this nature and, interestingly, they are contradictory. For the first, a Swedish naval captain has suggested that in the event of a European war, the

USSR would find it necessary to transport supplies by sea along its Baltic coast from Leningrad and other Baltic ports to its forces in Poland and the GDR. In these circumstances, NATO submarines would attempt to intercept the Soviet military transport. The Swedish captain conjectured that to do this in time of war, NATO submarines would prefer to utilize the external portions of Swedish territorial waters. This would permit them to move further up into the Baltic before attacking, presumably protected against the ASW elements of the Soviet Baltic Fleet by their location within Swedish waters. The captain went on to suggest that the Soviets realized that the Swedish navy would not have sufficient ASW resources to prevent NATO submarines from penetrating Swedish territorial waters, and they therefore were trying to convince the Swedish government to increase its ASW resources by demonstrating to Sweden the weakness of its ASW defenses.[48]

If this were the case, penetrations of Sweden's external territorial sea should have been sufficient. Penetration deep into Swedish internal waters or into its major naval base areas would not have been necessary. In addition, it does not seem an argument that would motivate extended operations after a Swedish protest, risking antagonizing the Swedish government. Finally, the entire thesis hangs on the plausibility of the USSR obeying wartime restrictions on operations in neutral Swedish waters while NATO disobeyed them. Swedish naval authorities allegedly expressed surprise following the discovery of Soviet submarines in Sundsvall harbor, and in other locations further north in the Baltic, on the grounds that it had been assumed that Soviet submarines "could not" operate in the northern Baltic. This was because international regulations required them to transit either Finnish or Swedish territorial waters to reach the area. If Soviet submarines disregarded such regulations in peacetime one can scarcely believe that they would feel compelled to obey them under wartime conditions.

The second suggestion was made by Colonel Jonathan

Alford, former deputy director of the International Institute of Strategic Studies in London. He also suggested that the Soviet submarine operations were intended to be noticed and that their purpose was to increase Swedish allocations for ASW. He argued, however, that the ultimate purpose was thereby to weaken the Swedish Air Force, because the increased allocations for ASW would have to be drawn from other portions of Swedish defense expenditures, particularly from those for the air force. Alford's argument was that in case of war Swedish submarine defenses would be irrelevant because the USSR did not intend to occupy Swedish land territory. The capabilities of the Swedish air force would be decisive, on the other hand, in determining the ability of Sweden to defend its airspace. Alford also believed that an early wartime requirement for the USSR would be the occupation of Norway's Atlantic coast air fields, and the USSR would want to use Swedish airspace to accomplish this. The Swedish air force would thus have to be defeated, and it would be to the Soviet's advantage to weaken the force.

> What I am very tentatively suggesting is that the Soviet Union may have embarked quite systematically on a massive deception plan. In peacetime, by such probing as we have seen, the Soviet Union has drawn attention to ASW weakness and difficulty. If that causes a massive diversion of funds away from other areas of defence (and especially air defence) to coastal defence, that could serve the Soviet Union well in the long run — if they have no intention of invading anyway! They might not in the least mind Swedish waters being well defended if they can proceed with relative impunity in other directions. This is not to say that their wartime plans do not include Spetsnaz and diversionary operations against the coast but that is a relatively low cost/ low risk operation intended simply in war to reinforce the message that Sweden would do better by not resisting — or that bad things could happen to Sweden if it did resist Soviet overflights.[49]

Conversely, one could argue that the Swedish demobilization of its ASW forces in the 1970s was a result of the large portion of Swedish defense expenditure that went toward the procurement of the Viggen attack aircraft. Although the submarine incursions may have produced a political atmosphere in Sweden that made it easier for the Social Democratic administration to obtain parliamentary approval in 1983 for the successor to the Viggen, the JAS aircraft, Swedish defense priorities continued to favor the procurement of expensive fighter aircraft over ASW systems. There was no substantial reallocation of Swedish defense expenditures as a result of the incursions.[50]

A more general purpose was also suggested by one commentator as "possibly one of the most important intentions of the country responsible for the submarine intrusions: to produce public confusion and to upset Swedish defense planning. Swedish politicians must find themselves uncertain: what goals should the Swedish defense forces actually have?"[51] The five years of submarine incursions must indeed have produced some rethinking about the traditional Swedish expectation that the nation would have sufficient time to bring its military forces from their low peacetime levels to full mobilization in the event of a European military crisis. If so, that was certainly not the intended purpose of the incursions.

Political

There have been suggestions that the submarine incursions were intended to apply political pressure, either to convince the Swedish government to increase some specific activity, to reduce another, or, more significantly, to change the basic nature of the Swedish security relationship with the USSR. Several general conclusions follow from these views. First, the submarine incursions by definition must have been decided on by the Soviet political leadership. It would be impossible in these circumstances to question whether the military was carrying them out under its own jurisdiction. It would also be less meaningful to speak of the "political costs" of the operations. If these were carried out for political purposes, Soviet decision makers must have considered in advance the risk that the outcome could be counterproductive, either in Sweden itself or on other issues. and decided that it was worth the risk. Finally, Soviet leaders must also have been willing to risk a major public debate on defense, security, and neutrality policies in Sweden. This would also be true as well if the submarine operations were carried out for military reasons. If they counted on little change, they were apparently correct. Several sharp outbursts of political invective took place, but there was no thoroughgoing debate. Over a span of 10 years, however, Swedish ASW capabilities would definitely be improved.

The earliest suggestion that the submarine incidents were intended as political pressure against Sweden came from Swedish Soviet specialist Ingmar Oldberg. He pointed out that the Soviet media had begun complaining in 1982 that Swedish procurement of jet engines for the forthcoming JAS aircraft was "a serious exception to Swedish neutrality policy" and that it "undermined the basis of Swedish neutrality." Writers in *Pravda* and other Soviet commentators also suggested that instead of arming, Sweden should insure its security by such measures as working for a Nordic nuclear-free zone. Oldberg also suggested that other political aims of the operations could be to attempt to weaken the Swedish public's confidence in the capability of its military services, to warn Sweden against any military cooperation with NATO, and, in general, to nudge Sweden toward a foreign policy that was more sympathetic to Soviet interests.[52] Insofar as the Swedish Viggen also had U.S. jet engines and earlier Swedish jet aircraft had British engines, this would seem more a post hoc rationalization on the part of the USSR afforded by the coincidence of Swedish government decisions on the JAS and the visit of U.S. Secretary of Defense Caspar Weinberger to Sweden in October 1981. In part, this visit did deal with Swedish weapon purchases from the United States, but the submarine events had started well before the JAS project appeared.

The suggestion that political motives were responsible for the Soviet submarine violations was also taken up in a report prepared by the small Swedish Liberal Party. The report pointed out that the longer the incursions continued, despite Swedish government protests, the more it seemed that the Soviet purposes were more extensive than implied by the SDC's conclusions.[53] Other Swedish political figures have pointed out that as the incidents reached their peak, Soviet political demands increased.[54] One of the factors suggesting political pressure is the coincidence between some of the major submarine incursions and political events. For instance, incursions occurred immediately after the release of the submarine commission's report, just after the visit of Foreign Minister Gromyko, and at the time of the sixtieth anniversary of USSR-Swedish diplomatic relations and the Swedish Foreign Ministry's invitation to the *Izvestia* columnist, Alexander Bovin, to Sweden.

With a rate of incursion from 1982 to 1984 of nearly one per week, such coincidence can, however, easily be assumed to be no more than that. Analysts, who believe that the incursions were carried out primarily for military purposes, also assume that political pressure was a secondary purpose, certainly once the operations were extensively disclosed to the public while being continued. For example, Colonel Alford suggested that

> after that, a clear political motivation must have intruded. The practice may have been more or less the same but its continuance after clear evidence of infringement and Swedish challenge conveys a very different message. . . . The message intended to be conveyed is: Let these things happen and we can continue to have normal relations; object to them too strenuously and life will get tough. . . . The message of successive submarine violations, not too subtly conveyed, was that Sweden was in no position to oppose Soviet de-

signs – and it would be better for Sweden that it did not oppose them. Bullying a neighbour into a submissive state of mind goes with what I take to be the current Soviet mood. If and when the time comes for the Soviet Union to violate Swedish neutrality in a big way, the Soviet calculation might be that Sweden, having been *unable* to resist in small matters, will be *unwilling* to resist in large ones.[55]

Alford suggested in particular that the USSR could be expected to demand the right to fly over Swedish airspace in time of war. Another specialist on Soviet military affairs commented that "The arrogance of the Soviet operations have been notable, to display that they can get away with it. They are happy to have the additional element of political bullying also." But it is Sweden's own policies for dealing with the incursions that has to a major degree permitted both the appearance of Swedish operational incapability and the impression that the Soviets "can get away with it."

The crux of the paradigm of political pressure was most clearly expressed by the Finnish researcher Tomas Ries. He noted that

The submarine intrusions have placed Sweden in the exceedingly difficult position of having to choose between outright confrontation with the USSR or acquiescence. . . .

Sweden's post-war security policy, like that of the other Nordic states, has been a delicate balance act, maintaining good relations with the USSR while retaining a maximum of independence of action backed up by a military deterrent against possible Soviet pressure. So far, the situation has never demanded that one objective be sacrificed for the other.

The submarine incursions appear deliberately designed to force just such a choice. If Sweden destroys or forces to the surface the intruding Soviet vessels, there would probably be very vicious short-term repercussions in the Baltic and a long-term chill in relations between the two countries. If Sweden permits the intruders to operate freely in the most sensitive restricted waters, psychologically the first step towards subservience to the Soviet Union will have been taken. In the latter case, the Soviet Union would have forced a key Nordic state to face up to the consequences of growing Soviet military superiority.[56]

The report on *Swedish Security Policy in the 1990s*, prepared by the Swedish Parliamentary Defense Committee and released in May 1985, reflects this situation in commenting on the submarine intrusions:

Swedish countermeasures taken in accordance with international law and current Swedish regulations can produce an acute conflict, for example if an intruding foreign unit were detained or injured, or if we refused to submit to demands from a foreign power.[57]

At the same time the committee noted the government's position:

Concerning underwater violations, the government and parliament have stated that incursions by foreign submarines into Swedish waters, in flagrant violation of the norms of international law, cannot be accepted under any circumstances. Sweden has made it clear that it is our firm intention to protect our territorial integrity and the inviolability of Swedish borders by all available means.[58]

This latter statement is the same as ones made in 1982 and 1983. Its application, however, has been less forceful than its phrasing. Writing somewhat more abstractly regarding Norway, Holst described its foreign policy as comprising three elements:

deterrence, reassurance, and insurance. . . . Reassurance is made up of a series of unilateral confidence-
building measures designed to communicate peaceful
intentions and avoid challenging vital Soviet security
interests during peacetime. . . . It is understood that
unmitigated deterrence could result in provocation,
much as maximizing reassurance could lead to appeasement and a single-minded pursuit of insurance to
escapism.[59]

Military/Operational Motives

The report of the SDC in 1983 concluded that "this submarine activity represents the preparatory phases of military
operational planning." It also reviewed various other suggestions that had been proposed and indicated why it did
not think these were reasonable. It rejected the suggestion
that the incursions might have been intended to provoke
Sweden to increase its ASW capabilities or to deliver particular political signals. Among the most likely tasks for the
submarine operations were explorations of the Swedish
coastal and archipelago areas and of Swedish ASW defenses, the testing of new systems, the development of operational tactics, the training of specialized units, and preparations for the laying and sweeping of mines. Mining by
submarines is considered particularly attractive because it
can be done covertly, before the initiation of hostilities. The
Parliamentary Defense Committee's report of 1986 extended this evaluation slightly: "The motives, which are difficult
to determine, can primarily be considered as different forms
of preparation for eventual crisis and war situations."[60] This
latter report noted that the submarine operations became
continually more provocative, that they included an increased number of units coordinated in individual operations, that they penetrated deeper into internal Swedish
waters, that they spread from a concentration in the summer months to year-round activities, and that they focused
on military bases, harbors, and restricted security zones.

Other details provided by military or other semiofficial sources noted that the submarine operations covered virtually the entire length of the Swedish coastline, that they often lasted weeks at a time, that they frequently accompanied Swedish military maneuvers, and that they paid particular attention to base defensive systems, not only peacetime base areas, but the Swedish navy's wartime locations as well. Admiral Tornberg noted that the navy could frequently discern more particular targets from the locations of the operations. He referred explicitly to visits by midget submarines to Swedish mine lines and other fixed bottom systems.[61] Midget submarines fitted with bow-mounted claws could also plant transponders (sonar response bouys fixed to the sea floor) to aid submarine navigation. Soviet midget submarines are fitted with this technology. Such a task would in itself, however, only be a preliminary step to some other mission and could serve a wide variety of subsequent missions. The Swedish commander in chief's judgment was that "The magnitude of the activities and the risks that the foreign power is apparently prepared to take indicate that the motives are not solely of a limited nature."[62]

One of the more exotic suggestions was included in Arkady Shevchenko's disclosures. He claimed that the USSR was preparing to hide its nuclear submarines in Swedish waters in time of crisis.[63] That certainly could not be the reason for the operations within Sweden's major naval base areas. One would not "hide" assets as valuable as ballistic missile submarines within Sweden's two major — and shallow — naval harbor basins. Even the older Soviet Golf-class missile submarines would for the most part not be able to transit many of the archipelago channels even if they traveled on the surface — and certainly not if submerged.[64] The suggestion therefore seems implausible. One could argue that if someone wanted to hide ballistic missile submarines in neutral territory it would be necessary to destroy any local ASW forces. One would also want to know the extent of Swedish and Norwegian ASW capabilities and whether in fact it was possible to hide the submarines successfully in enemy territory. The British naval expert Michael MccGwire has suggested that the intrusions in deeper Norwegian waters could be reconnaissance related to the deployment of older Soviet missiles submarines, bringing them within range of the European theater, whereas the pattern of operations in Sweden suggested that the Soviets were rehearsing missions against key installations.

In a television interview at the time of the Hårsfjärden events in 1982, U.S. Admiral Stansfield Turner suggested that the most reasonable way to think about the reasons for the submarine operations was to think of "standard operating procedures."[65] The Soviet Union has some 30 conventionally powered submarines in its Baltic Fleet, and these have to be given something to do.[66] Admiral Turner did not think the submarines were on intelligence assignments in the traditional sense. He suggested rather that they were on exercises with the purpose of making themselves knowledgeable about Swedish internal waters and terrain. They would be training for wartime missions to neutralize the Swedish navy by blockading the major naval bases. In an eventual wartime situation, the Soviet navy would not want to have to worry about the Swedish fleet, and the simplest way to do that would be to keep the Swedish ships bottled up in their bases. Because of the enclosed nature of the two main Swedish naval bases, that might be feasible. U.S. Department of State analyst Dale Herspring quotes an unusual East German naval article on strategic naval issues in which the author discusses "some peculiarities of the struggle for *Seeherrschaft* in enclosed naval areas of operations," that is, in the Baltic. The article discusses destroying and blockading an opponent's forces in their bases, blockading the entrances to or exits from enclosed areas, and destroying key installations. It further emphasizes the importance of being able to commence operations the moment hostilities begin.

Porschel's comments on the attitude of neutrals suggest that he expects the Swedes to adopt a more forthcoming stance if the Pact is winning. It is not clear,
however, whether this would be the result of a volun-
tary act by the Swedes or of Pact pressure to support
Soviet actions. . . . Porschel's remarks . . . may also indicate that in a NATO-Warsaw Pact confrontation, the
Pact has plans for at least containing the Swedes.[67]

If one looks at Soviet doctrinal writings, in which the
formal operational limits are often set out in great legalistic
detail, one quickly finds the context in which the submarine
operations fit.

Soviet military and naval warfare is planned and predi-
cated on the geostrategic basis of theaters of war (teatr
voyny-TV) and theaters of military operations (teatr
voyennykh deystviy-TVD). In Soviet military thinking,
a theater of war is comprised of two or more (rarely,
perhaps, one) theaters of military operations. Theaters
of military operations, in turn, are composed, albeit
less formally, of zones of military operations.
   The geographic dimension of a TV is continental.
It is the territory and adjoining air and sea space of any
one continent on which, according to the Soviet General Staff, "hostilities may develop." Traditionally, but not
exclusively, this is Europe. . . .
   The General Staff Academy Dictionary definition
of "TVD" is "TEATR VOYENNYKH DEYSTVIY (the-
ater of military operations) – a particular territory, together with the associated air space and sea areas, including islands (archipelagos), within whose limits a
known part of the armed forces of the country (or coalition) operates in wartime, engaged in strategic missions which ensue from the war plan. A theater of operations may be ground, maritime, or intercontinental.
According to their military-political and economic importance, theaters of operations are classified as main
or secondary. . . .
   It is widely and well known that TVDs are the key

geographical construct for operational-strategical Soviet and Warsaw Pact ground, air and air defense operation, that is, both in training maneuvers and in the event of genuine combat operations. However, there has been, practically speaking, almost no deliberate discussion in the West of a closely similar theater concept which has long and often been reflected in Soviet discussions of their own naval strategy and warfare. Yet the Soviets, for years, have been applying the same fundamental strategic concepts to naval warfare as they have to continental warfare. This common referential practice continues. The Soviets refer often to the "morskoi teatr voyennykh deystviy" – the naval (or maritime) theater of military operations. . . .

The 1965 General Staff Academy Dictionary (as based in part on the 1957 Naval Operational-Tactical Manual) defines the "MTVD" "MORSKOY (OKEANSKIY) TEATR VOYENNYKH DEYSTVIY (i.e., naval or maritime [or oceanic] theater of military operations, or alternatively "theater of naval operations") – The water and air space of one or several seas (or oceans), together with its islands and coastlines, where naval operations may take place in wartime."[68]

According to the best description available, the bottom quarter of Sweden's land territory and the lower half of the Baltic, together with most of continental Europe, fall within the western TVD in Soviet operational planning. The largest part of Sweden's land territory and the upper Baltic fall within the northwestern TVD, which also includes Norway, Finland, and the Barents and Norwegian seas. The Baltic is not considered an "oceanic" theater and is split between those two TVDs.[69]

The General Staff Academy Dictionary even provides a definition of a "Zakrytyi" MTVD or an "enclosed theatre of naval operations," and goes on to define some 15 different functional or positional zones within a TVD. The Soviet Ministry of Defense has established the priority of naval missions as follows:

- delivering strategic nuclear weapons strikes,
- destroying enemy naval forces at sea and in port,
- disrupting enemy and protecting one's own sea routes,
  - aiding ground forces in continental TVDs,
  - conducting and repelling amphibious assaults,
  - transporting troops and supplies, and
  - evacuating troops and supplies.[70]

Naval operations that support ground operations in coastal regions are referred to as *"deistviia voenno-morsko-go flota na primorskikh napravleniiakh,"* as "naval activities in coastal areas." Tasks under this term include anticarrier operations, the transport of troops and matériel, the disruption of enemy shipping, amphibious operations, anti-amphibious operations, and the defense of friendly sea transport and lines of communication. Whatever one's interpretations of the way in which Soviet theater forces would first go to war, the themes of surprise and covertness and of the oft-cited "battle for the first salvo," are leading and persistent elements.[71]

Most important for the considerations in this study is the definition of one of the 14 specific kinds of Soviet naval theater operations, the "Preparation of an MTVD." As defined by the naval and general staffs in the *Dictionary of Basic Military Terms*,

> This is an entire "system of measures" undertaken in peacetime and in wartime, within the limits of an MTVD, to create or lead to conditions favorable to Soviet combat operations and to hinder enemy operations. It includes building bases, equipping facilities with war and survival material, creating dispersal routes, points, cover, and support facilities, deployment along coastlines of technical facilities for observations, communications navigation and radio reconnaissance. It includes taking ASW, AAW, and anti-mine, anti-nuclear and anti-landing preparatory measures.

Also includes the creation of technical and material reserves.[72]

It is this "preparation of the MTVD," or preparing a theater for military action, that some analysts consider as the cause of the submarine operations in Swedish waters. Whether the Soviet Baltic Fleet would seek to pass into the Atlantic in a time of war in Europe or is intended to remain behind to secure the sea for its own operations, it would be concerned with the Swedish navy and coastal facilities. It is on these grounds, Michael MccGwire explains, that the USSR has always been interested in Sweden's coastline.

Their northern flank is the Baltic. They must be sure that it is secure – consequently they are concerned about the Swedish coastline in that context.

They want that coastline to be blind in terms of sensors. They do not want radar and underwater sensors reporting on where they are. Certainly they would be challenging Western units if they did operate in those waters. But they would also be going ashore to pull out radar stations and rip up sonar sensors and things like that.

The idea that these coastal operations are a precursor to an actual invasion, a physical takeover of Sweden – is to my mind nonsensical. The Soviets are going to be very short of forces if war comes. And the last thing they'd want to do is get bogged down in an unnecessary war on the northern flank of their main theatre of operations.

What they want to do is make sure that Sweden is really neutral, and that it does not have sensor systems or anything else which can affect the operations. And if they can neutralize it at a fairly cheap cost – with special forces and other ways like that – that is all they need to do. . . .

If war is in the distant future, they don't have to be too worried about preparing that theatre, knowing exactly where they have to go and what's happening in it.

But if war is seen to be more likely, clearly there is more pressure to ensure that they are on top of the operation that they have to carry out in their theatre.

And this is I think what we saw.

Last year (1983) there were multiple operations — these were not reconnaissance operations, they were more like exercises and contingency plans — and I see that as reflecting a general concern in Russia, which you can pick up in what they were writing from 1981 on — that they see war as being more likely, the general international situation making war more likely than, say, in the late seventies.[73]

Writing a year later, MccGwire stated:

The Baltic constitutes the northern flank of the Western TVD which is the main TVD of the main theater, where military success has to be assured if the Soviet Union is not to lose. The Swedish archipelago defines the northern perimeter of the Baltic MTVD and the Soviets have two kinds of interest in this coastline: to prevent it being used to their disadvantage; and to use selected parts of it for their own purposes. Thorough peacetime reconnaissance is important to both missions, which would have to be discharged at the very onset of war.[74]

MccGwire explicitly rejected the suggestion that the submarine operations could have been intended to apply political pressure on Sweden.

One . . . has to identify the benefits that would have justified the risk of incurring further political costs (both in relation to Sweden and to public opinion in Europe that was being wooed for INF), by sharply increasing the number and boldness of these operations. The idea that the higher level of incursions was designed to apply political pressure on Sweden is unpersuasive. . . . There are many ways of using one's armed forces to bring "pressure" on a neighbor, but infesting its waters with midget submarines that get detected and risk being surfaced or destroyed is not one of them. The political costs were foreseeable and duly incurred, namely Swedish political truculence and a spurt of investment in anti-submarine measures.[75]

MccGwire thought that the USSR would not feel compelled to destroy the Swedish fleet – but that it would want to be certain that the Swedish navy was not able to be used and that NATO could not make use of it. As the submarine incursions continued, the landing of Soviet *Spetsnaz* in wartime – to destroy particular coastal defense facilities and to perform the kinds of missions MccGwire mentions – was widely discussed. A brigade of these units, such as assigned to the Baltic Fleet, could probably field as many as 100 individual *Spetsnaz* teams. Their targets would be ship and submarine bases, airfields, command and intelligence centers, communications facilities, radar sites, and ports and harbors. They would carry out their operations immediately before hostilities began.[76] Swedish military sources have added minesweeping and the destruction of coastal artillery defenses to these prospective missions. It is reckoned that 70 passes of an attack aircraft would be required to destroy a unit of three coastal artillery guns. Placing a string of destructive charges on each gun barrel by an attack diver would achieve the same result. It is assumed that operational plans for the northwestern TVD include contingencies for combat operations against Sweden as well.[77] Soviet amphibious operations also would be expected in the Baltic.

Elsewhere, in discussing Soviet naval missions in the Arctic and the adjacent northwestern TVDs – which are more relevant to the Soviet operations in Norwegian waters – MccGwire makes several points that are also relevant to some degree to the Swedish coastal incursions. He states that the Soviets' primary strategic objective in the Arctic

TVD is to deny Western forces access to the area, so that the area can be used without hindrance for Soviet military purposes. The most important of these purposes is the protection of the submarine ballistic missile component of the USSR's Northern Fleet. By 1975, the Western term, "command of the sea," had been reinstated in Soviet military terminology and was considered an essential precondition for the success of the strategic mission of the SSBN force. In Soviet discussions of the concept, which MccGwire points out are in general terms and not tied to any specific area, three points are of particular relevance: the need to prepare extensively in peacetime for the task of gaining command in war, the assertion that the West will be seeking to gain command at the very outset of a war, and the value of controlling adjacent coastal areas.[78] It is noteworthy that in April 1986, the USSR carried out naval maneuvers off the north Norwegian coast that culminated in a landing exercise less than 20 km from the Soviet-Norwegian border. It is assumed by Norwegian defense authorities that the exercise simulated an amphibious landing in the north Trondelag area.[79]

McccGwire's reasoning about Soviet intentions concerning the Swedish coast in the case of war seems the most plausible. It is similar to Admiral Turner's, only somewhat more detailed. For this writer, only one problem remains with MccGwire's interpretation: his assumption about the timing of the submarine incursions is not plausible. McccGwire accepts the Soviet contention that war with the West—either in Europe or a nuclear war—was more likely, even imminent, after 1980 or 1981. The most senior statements came from Andropov, Ustinov, and Ogarkov. Soviet officials claimed that "the United States was driving the world toward a nuclear catastrophe," that the United States "was preparing a first strike against the USSR," and that "the world is pushed closer and closer to a nuclear abyss." The campaign culminated in a June 3, 1984 statement in *Krasnaya Zvezda* (Red Star) that the West German army "is bracing itself for aggression jointly with the U.S. armed forces against the Soviet Union and other Warsaw Treaty States." These statements continued until the period in the fall of 1984 when Foreign Minister Gromyko was meeting with Secretary of State George Shultz and President Ronald Reagan to plan the renewal of arms control negotiations with the United States.[80]

MccGwire believes that this Soviet perception drove their war preparation time down from perhaps 18 months to 6 months. There was, however, no greater likelihood of war and it is impossible to believe that Soviet military and political leaders thought there was. In addition, Moscow ended its campaign on the themes that "war is coming" and "the U.S. is driving the world to nuclear war" virtually overnight in October 1984, before the U.S. presidential elections, when Moscow decided to resume negotiations with the Reagan administration. Although not the most important piece of evidence, the abrupt end of this campaign is additional support for the view that the Soviet leadership did not believe war to be imminent at any time during 1980–1984. If the USSR had feared war, there should have been many other more important strategic indicators than the submarine incursions.

There are, however, other indications of revised Soviet military planning for war in Europe that may be more relevant. Many analysts of Soviet military affairs now assume that around 1975 the Soviet General Staff came to the conclusion that a war in Central Europe could remain at the conventional level, without escalating to nuclear war. It then instituted a series of organizational and operational changes in the late 1970s designed to facilitate the use of previously nuclear-oriented, general purpose forces in a conventional war.[81] In addition, for the first time in the postwar era, Soviet general purpose ground and naval forces based in the border military districts and in Eastern Europe were directed to assume increased alert levels. Thus the Soviet campaign in 1982–1984 about the imminence of war may rather have served as a cover for its own doctrinal changes, already decided on and already being instituted. If the

USSR had revised its war plans, it is also reasonable that it had to demonstrate that the plans were valid by exercising them. One must again note, however, that the only place in which changes of this magnitude in Soviet peacetime operations were apparent was in the submarine operations in Swedish waters. Shipdays-at-sea of the Soviet Northern Fleet also increased substantially, from fewer than 100 per year in 1976 to nearly 900 per year in 1985.

MccGwire's analysis nevertheless stands in marked contrast to the more general references by Swedish government officials to the increased importance of the overall Nordic region. The most specific of these was given by the Swedish defense minister in January 1984:

> Tensions are concentrated primarily in the North Cape — because the USSR has its most important naval base on the Kola Peninsula — and in the Southern Baltic. If there should be war, NATO will block the Baltic exits. The USSR is concerned that NATO should not be able to utilize the Baltic and they take that as the starting point for their plans. The submarine incidents should be seen in that perspective.[82]

If, however, NATO only wants to block the Baltic exits, and the USSR is concerned that NATO should not be able to enter and utilize the Baltic, direct interaction of Soviet and NATO fleets in the Baltic could be avoided. In addition, it is difficult to understand how Soviet operations against Swedish naval bases would help them keep NATO out of the Baltic.

More recently a Swedish analyst has updated this North Atlantic U.S.-USSR naval context for the submarine events by introducing the Reagan administration's maritime strategy, publicized in January 1986, which emphasizes a more forward projection of U.S. naval forces in the Norwegian sea.[83] All the available evidence indicates, however, that the submarine incursions were initiated long before this strategy was formulated. Another analysis by a Swedish military strategist is in essence not much different from MccGwire's, though it remains on a general level and does not go into particulars. It is given a twist, however, by its phrasing that "It is fully natural and obvious that war preparations are taking place. It would be a breach of duty on the part of the Soviet General Staff if they didn't carry out such activities."[84] The new Swedish chief of staff-designate carried this logic a step further in correcting his remark that the submarine incursions were being carried out by the USSR. He questioned whether the submarine operations were "preparations for attack" and suggested instead that they were "defensive": "they can equally well . . . be defensive, namely to assure themselves that there doesn't exist any threat against them: i.e., they have a great need to feel secure and therefore they do these kinds of investigations."[85]

Other analysts go further than MccGwire and assume that the USSR would make major landings on Swedish soil at Sundsvall to cross over to reach Trondheim in Norway. This is something that NATO apparently does not expect and for which it has not planned.[86] This could include a means of attacking the newly located prepositioned supplies for U.S. forces in Norway. MccGwire also is willing to conceive of a Soviet landing at Sundsvall, but only in the case of an extended European war. If the USSR intended putting ashore land forces at Sundsvall, the Swedish navy certainly would have to be put out of action. Yet it is even more difficult to assume that the USSR was actively preparing for a long European war in 1980–1984, although once the submarine incursion missions were in full swing, one can imagine that an attempt was made to fulfill as many military planning requirements as possible.

Two authors have proposed explanations for the submarine operations that do address the question of why the years 1980–1984 were chosen. Both did this by considering the effect of events in Poland on Soviet and the WTO's planning. Örjan Berner, a Swedish diplomat, suggested that the USSR had to consider alternative means of protecting its flank in the Baltic as Poland's performance in possible Warsaw Pact operations became more uncertain.[87] Because Sweden would in no way conceivably intervene in Warsaw Pact military operations in case of war, irrespective of Poland's contribution, it is not clear why a presumptive Soviet need to strengthen its Baltic flank should require Soviet operations in Sweden.

Robert Weinland, a U.S. naval analyst, proposed a very different explanation. His first point is that the USSR would have a great interest in occupying and using airfields in southern Norway early in a major European war. He also notes that the Soviet military apparently had a rudimentary plan during World War II for crossing southern and central Sweden, beginning with large-scale amphibious landings at one or more of six potential sites. He points out that many of the submarine incursions have occurred in these same areas, as well as near the major Swedish naval bases. He therefore believes that the incursions suggest increased Soviet interest in "the forces and facilities in Sweden that would in the first instance bar, and in the second facilitate, Soviet use of central and southern Sweden as an avenue of attack into Southern Norway."[88] A factor that would explain increased Soviet interest in such operations would be the establishment of a new requirement, the post-1975 emphasis on planning for conventional war in Europe. Weinland argues that the conventional scenario that would guide the 1981–1985 period was being articulated in 1980–1981 as the Polish crisis was coming to a head. Until then, Polish forces had played a prominent role in Soviet plans to close the Baltic approaches in time of war. Weinland believes that the USSR was forced to find a substitute for the Polish contribution, hence the submarine incursions in Sweden.

As in the case of Berner's suggestion, Weinland posits not simply a substitution for Polish forces but an entirely different kind of operation to make the substitution.

Weinland does not suggest that there was any previous thought of using Polish forces for operations through Sweden, or that the previous Polish contributions to Warsaw Pact operations had ever required prior submarine operations in Swedish waters. It should be much simpler for Soviet forces to take on the Baltic-related mission that had previously been assigned to Polish forces rather than to seek an entire new mode of operations.

In summary, MccGwire and Admiral Turner probably provide the most likely approximations of the military purpose of the incursions. Both serve to supply more detail to the SDC's conclusion that the operations were of a "military operational" character. The introduction of the Polish factor certainly fits the years 1980–1984, yet it seems to involve Sweden unnecessarily. To make a judgment as to whether the motives for the incursions were solely political or solely military is difficult, if not impossible. They certainly could have been both. Once the incursions developed, they probably served both purposes simultaneously, whatever the original intentions. Political pressure probably would not have been intended for peacetime – during which it was apparently counterproductive – but [for use against] the Swedish government in wartime. In his treatise on *The Use of Force in International Relations*, the British political scientist C. S. Northedge wrote,

> Failure to make clear to a hostile state the borderline between what you are prepared to tolerate and what you must resist may lead to a situation in which the opponent does not know what your "point of no return" is, or whether you will allow yourself to be pushed to it or beyond it. In these circumstances a war which perhaps neither side wanted, can come about. . . .[89]

Whether the Soviet political goals were achieved, only time and the nature of ultimate Soviet political intentions in Europe in the decades to come will tell.

Conclusion

Between 1980 and 1986 – depending on the accounting criteria used – the Soviet Union carried out some 100 to 200
submarine incursions within Swedish territorial waters.
Many of these took place deep in internal waters, often in
the immediate proximity of major Swedish naval bases and
within the perimeters of restricted security zones. In other
cases, the operations took place within the harbors of Sweden's major cities. The operations often included coordina-
tion of the activities of several submarines and midget submarines within the same area. The best understanding of
the purpose of these submarine operations was that they
represented some kind of exercise – maneuvers of specialized units – and contingency planning. In the case of war,
such units, among other possible functions, would presumably destroy Swedish coastal defense installations and in
one way or another interdict the operations of the Swedish
navy. That these incursions have continued over an extended period of time has led to suggestions that their intention
may have been either primarily or secondarily to exert political pressure on Sweden. The aim of such pressure would
have been to effect changes in Swedish neutrality or foreign
policies or to force Sweden to acquiesce to Soviet military
movements within its territory both in times of peace and
of war.

The Swedish government protested to the USSR
against the incursions in strong terms, in diplomatic notes
of protest in 1981 and 1983, in public statements, and via
private emissaries to the Soviet government. The incidents
nevertheless continued and, in all likelihood, increased in
frequency and severity following the Swedish protests.
These events received some attention in the Western media
at the time of two of the major incidents, the stranding of a
Whisky-class submarine in Karlskrona in October 1981 and
the Hårsfjärden incidents in October–November 1982. Otherwise, there has been little or no analysis of the events in
terms of the basic premises of Soviet foreign policy and

behavior and absolutely no analysis of them in the context of the security policies and responses of the country that is the victim of the incursions, in this case a neutral and non-aligned state. The Swedish government has termed the sequences of submarine incursions the most serious violation of its neutrality since the end of World War II.

The Soviet government has rejected all Swedish protest notes and denied all responsibility for the incursions. It has repeatedly informed Sweden that it desires only good neighborly relations based on mutual respect and on respect for international borders. On occasion, it has offered these reassurances at the very time that a sequence of submarine incursions was taking place and at the same time that it was urging Sweden to act with greater "reality." If better relations between the two do not exist, the USSR claims the fault lies with Sweden, not with the USSR. The senior Soviet political leadership unquestionably knew of the operations, but considered them important enough to continue—despite Swedish protests and the strategic warning that they provided to Sweden and to other states.

Other external Soviet military programs, in Afghanistan or in Africa, can be documented by the international community, properly credited to the Soviet Union, and assessed in terms of the goals of Soviet foreign policy. The submarine operations in Swedish waters are both covert and denied. From 1983–1986, they also came to be accompanied by a Swedish government policy of avoiding attribution to the USSR and withholding information about the events. Instead of taking actions that would increase the transparency surrounding the events, this policy permitted the entire affair to take on a semi-surrealistic quality. The interpretation of Soviet foreign policy has always been difficult. In this case, the Swedish government's restraint deprived the international community of important and unambiguous evidence of the extent of the Soviet Union's willingness to pressure a neighboring state in times of peace and of evidence that also has major implications regarding Soviet intentions in war.

The operations are the first Soviet military-political initiatives against a Western European state since the Berlin crises of 1960–1961. The provisional, more exploratory stages of the operations apparently began well before 1980, that is, before the deterioration of Soviet-U.S. political relations and the demise of "détente." The Soviet government has continued the operations at the same time as it has pressed a public campaign for a Nordic Nuclear-Free Zone, constantly referred to the Baltic as a "Sea of Peace" in its public statements, and participated in the Conference on Security-Building and Disarmament in Europe. Indeed, this conference last took place in Stockholm, the capital of the country against which the submarine operations have been directed. There could hardly be Soviet actions that more succinctly demonstrate its attitudes toward "confidence-building measures."

Notes

A Note to the Reader: The titles of original Swedish, Norwegian, and Danish sources have been translated into English. The names of Sweden's two major daily newspapers, *Dagens Nyheter* and *Svenska Dagbladet* have been abbreviated to *DN* and *SvD* respectively. The Swedish navy's journal, *Marin Nytt* (*Navy News*), is indicated by *MN*.

Introduction

1. In the highly classified project Holystone, the United States carried out a program in which U.S. submarines entered Soviet territorial waters on intelligence-collecting missions for perhaps as long as 15 years. The program was first disclosed by the *Washington Post* in January 1974 (Laurence Stern, "U.S. Spying in Soviet Waters," *Washington Post*, January 4, 1974) and then in greater detail in the *New York Times* in May 1975 (Seymour Hersh, "Submarines of U.S. Stage Spy Missions Inside Soviet Waters," *New York Times*, May 25, 1975). It is not known exactly when these operations began or when they were terminated. Writing in 1975, Hersh stated that the operations had been in progress "for nearly 15 years," which would imply that the operations began in 1960, and that "Holystone was authorized in the early 1960s." In his diary entry for November 12, 1959, George Kistiakowsky, science adviser to President Dwight D. Eisenhower, however, recorded the following remarks:

> Special intelligence briefings on Soviet naval activities
> . . . . There was also a very interesting account of the ways in
> which our navy gets intimate information on the Soviet naval
> activities, but that is so hush-hush I can't put it down on
> paper. Someday, it will make a very exciting news story.

In the volume of these diaries published in 1976, Kistiakowsky
added the comment, "It did in 1975," alluding to the Hersh story.
See George B. Kistiakowsky, *A Scientist at the White House*
(Cambridge, Mass.: Harvard University Press, 1976), 153. The
purpose of the U.S. submarine incursions was reportedly to moni-
tor Soviet submarine-launched ballistic missile (SLBM) tests, to
record engine "signatures" of Soviet submarines, and to perform
other intelligence tasks. Some of the submarines even entered
Vladivostok harbor for these intelligence-gathering purposes. It
is assumed that the USSR knew of these operations because of
accidents that occurred within Soviet waters during the program,
but there is no public knowledge that the USSR ever protested to
the United States about the operations.

    2. The FCMA treaty commits Finland to defend the USSR
should West Germany or any state allied with West Germany
attack the USSR by way of Finland. The treaty also commits
Finland to consult with the USSR if the threat of such an attack
is noted by both parties of the treaty. The original treaty was
signed in April 1948 and was recently renewed by Finland for the
third time, so that the treaty now extends beyond the year 2000.

    3. Mogens Esperssen, "The Security-Political History of the
Baltic," *The Baltic: Yesterday – Today – Tomorrow* (Copenhagen:
Forsvarets Oplysnings-og Velfaerdstjeneste, 1982), 5–15.

    4. Ibid., 10. This was effectively a continuation of previous
Soviet policy. As early as November 1939, Soviet Foreign Minister Vyacheslav Molotov informed his German counterpart Joa-
chim von Ribbentrop that the USSR was not uninterested in the
Baltic approaches and asked for Soviet naval bases in Jutland.
Immediately after the German occupation of Denmark and Norway in April 1940, the USSR notified Germany of its wish to
participate in joint control of the Danish straits. Stalin repeated
the request for Soviet bases in Jutland at Tehran in 1943, and in
1945 at Yalta he requested the creation of a Soviet-protected state
of Kiel, which by way of the Kiel Canal would have made the
USSR a coastal state of the North Sea.

Chapter 1

1. The series of data for 1970 to 1980 was released in Defense Staff Information Section, *Incidents: 1980*, April 15, 1981, mimeographed, 11 pages. The data for the subsequent years are extracted from analogous Swedish Defense staff annual releases:

- *Incidents: 1981*, June 21, 1982, mimeographed;
- *Incidents: 1982*, June 2, 1983, mimeographed;
- *Incidents: 1983*, June 19, 1984, mimeographed;
- *Incidents During the Fourth Quarter 1984, Including a Brief Summary of Incidents for All of 1984*, January 31, 1985, mimeographed;
- *Incidents During the Fourth Quarter 1985, Including a Brief Summary for All of 1985*, January 24, 1986, mimeographed; and,
- *Incidents During the Third Quarter 1986*, October 20, 1986, mimeographed.

2. Submarine Defense Commission, *Countering the Submarine Threat: Submarine Violations and Swedish Security Policy*, no. 13 (Stockholm: Swedish Official Reports Series [SOU], 1983).

3. The 1984 Defense Committee, *Sweden's Security Policy: Entering the 1980s*, no. 23 (Stockholm: SOU, 1985): 43.

4. K. Captain Cay Holmberg, "We Must Accept Foreign Submarines in Swedish Waters," *MN*, no. 2 (1980): 2. Holmberg described a Swedish Defense staff commentary that "there have only been a few submarines that have violated Swedish territory recently" following an incident on March 12, 1980 as "nearly comic" on the grounds that it was impossible for the Defense staff to know what the incidence level really was. There was also a question of almost prohibitive criteria. Before 1982 a visual identification by two naval officers was necessary to satisfy the requirements for an assured indication of a submarine violation. A composite of technical indications was ruled out. This should, presumably, have produced a very strong bias against registering assured violations. Finally, senior naval officers had apparently scoffed at submarine reports from field officers for some years. This led to the situation in which such reports were not included in the count of violations—and that count was presumably low

because field officers didn't report indications unless a submarine
was absolutely visible.

5. Moderate Party Report, *Countering the Submarine
Threat*, September 1982, p. 4.

6. Erik Lidén, "Researchers Skeptical About New Antisubmarine Weapons," *SvD*, September 30, 1985.

7. Lars Christiansson and Roger Magnergård, "The Navy
Can Only Defend a Limited Portion of the Coast," *SvD*, November
5, 1985. The quotation is by Admiral Claes Tornberg. Only a
single member of the Swedish press noticed the obvious consequences of such an assessment, and it received no further public
comment:

> the Swedish navy lacks adequate capacity today to detect
> foreign submarines, even if by chance it should have ships in
> the area. This means in turn that the number of submarine
> violations are much higher than what the statistics indicate.

Fredrik Braconier, "Confrontation at Hårsfjärden: Credulity Versus Grim Reality," *SvD*, November 5, 1985.

8. Moderate Party Report, *Strengthen Antisubmarine Defenses*, September 10, 1985, p. 7. See also Carl Bildt, "From Clear
Speech to 'Eventual Possibility,'" *SvD*, November 14, 1985.

Chapter 2

1. "Japan Hunts Unidentified Submarine," *DN*, August 27,
1983.

2. In September 1984, *Mainichi Shimbum* defense correspondent Yoshihisa Komori obtained verification from sources in the
Japanese Foreign Ministry and Japanese Self-Defense Forces of
midget submarine activity, presumably Soviet, in Japanese waters and reported this in an article in the newspaper *Mainichi
Shimbun* (personal communication).

3. The description was given by an officer of the Japanese
Self-Defense Forces on a Swedish television newscast in 1984.

4. "Similar Tracks Off Japan," *SvD*, August 4, 1985. The Jap-
anese authorities chose to withhold photographs of the tracks.
See also Robert C. Toth, "Soviet Naval Challenge to U.S. Grows in
Pacific," *International Herald Tribune*, July 30, 1985.

5. Lars Christiansson and Roger Magnergård, "Soviet Photograph of a Midget Submarine Published in *Pravda*," *SvD*, November 19, 1984. No comment was offered regarding the results of these investigations.

6. "Italians Issue a Protest Over Intrusion by Sub," *New York Times*, March 2, 1982.

7. "Submarine Hunt Near Greenland," *DN*, July 16, 1983; Marian Leighton, "Soviet Strategy Towards Northern Europe and Japan," *Survey* 27, no. 118–119 (Autumn–Winter 1983): 132; editorial in *Berlingske Tidende* (Copenhagen), July 19, 1983.

8. Richard Eder, "Yellow Sub Increases Concern by Danes Over Soviet Maneuvers," *International Herald Tribune*, December 16, 1981. These exercises and the more or less continuous Soviet naval presence off Danish coasts prompted a high-level Danish security official to state, "We put questions to the Russians, we say, 'Why do you come so close?' They say, 'This is not a threat to you, but we are expanding our naval capabilities, and we have every right to be here. But it is not a threat to you.'" This is very different from the 1950s and 1960s when the USSR used to complain bitterly about U.S. military maneuvers close to Soviet territory by asking how the U.S. government would feel if the USSR carried out maneuvers close to U.S. shores. In 1967, a Soviet statement claimed that "the very fact of U.S.-Japanese exercises close to Soviet shores cannot be regarded as anything but a premeditated, organized provocative military demonstration," Tass, May 13, 1967.

9. Eugene Kozicharow, "Soviet Buildup in Baltic Troubles Danes," *Aviation Week and Space Technology* 109, no. 20 (November 13, 1978): 49–50, 55. The *Aviation Week and Space Technology* article includes an informative map showing the westward shift in the locations of Soviet amphibious exercises: 1957 on the USSR's own Baltic coast, 1963 in Poland, 1970 in the DDR, and 1976 in the DDR's Rügen, just south of Denmark's Zealand coast. The 1977 Taga exercise returned to the Soviet Baltic coast, while the June and September 1980 Waffenbruderschaft exercise was again directed at the DDR's Rügen. In 1981, the Zapad 81 maneuvers included amphibious landings in Poland. The map also indicates the location of Soviet naval patrol areas just off the coasts of Denmark and West Germany.

10. Ibid.

11. Norwegian Ministry of Defense, "Foreign Submarines in

Norwegian Waters" (Oslo: Press and Information Section, April 1983). See also Johan J. Holst, "Coast States Defense Against Submarines in Peace," *NUPI Notat* (Norwegian Institute of International Affairs, June 1984); Admiral R. Breivik, "Foreign Submarines in Our Waters," *Horten*, June 13, 1983, mimeographed, 46 pages. It is clear that the "230 alleged violations of Norwegian territorial waters by unidentified submarines since 1970," which is quoted by Marian Leighton and for which she references an Agence France-Presse dispatch, is congruent with the total number of observations—including false ones—and is therefore at least two times too high. See Marian Leighton, "Soviet Strategy Towards Northern Europe and Japan," 128–129.

12. Knut Falchenberg, "Hunt for Soviet Submarine Continues by the Navy," *Aftenposten*, July 2, 1983. One would otherwise have to conclude that the Norwegian navy is using depth charges against echoes and spurious contacts and that ASW sensor equipment carried by the Orions would not be performing better.

13. Norwegian Ministry of Defense, "Analysis of Operations in Sunnhordland, April 27–May 6, 1983," August 12, 1983, mimeographed, 37 pages.

14. Erik Magnusson, "Norwegian Commander in Chief on Submarine Violations: Sovereignty Undermined," *DN*, January 13, 1986.

15. Fred Hiatt, "Oslo Opted to Spare Sub, Norwegian General Says," *Washington Post*, June 4, 1983. A briefer report, "Officer Asserts Norway Spared Russian Sub," appeared in the *International Herald Tribune* on June 5–6, 1983.

16. "Additional Submarines Observed Previously," *Bergens Tidende*, April 28, 1983.

17. The June 1985 *Los Angeles Times* story that was later reported in the July 1985 *International Herald Tribune* (Robert C. Toth, "Soviet Naval Challenge to U.S. Grows in Pacific," *International Herald Tribune*, July 30, 1985), which referred to "crawler marks, similar to those found in Swedish and *Norwegian* fjords" is wrong in regard to Norway. Norwegian authorities have never reported finding such tracks.

18. Björn Lindahl, "Fortified Troms is Norway's Gate in the North: Provocations are Avoided," *DN*, December 12, 1983.

19. Daniel Heradstveit and G. Matthew Bonham, "Decision Making in the Face of Uncertainty," *NUPI Rapport*, no. 56 (Norwegian Institute of International Affairs, June 1981).

20. Writing in 1981, a U.S. researcher, Kirsten Amundsen, reported that only seven violations of Norwegian territorial waters by Soviet surface vessels had been reported in the Norwegian press between 1945 and 1978, a period of 33 years. See Kirsten Amundsen, *Norway, NATO, and the Forgotten Soviet Challenge* (Berkeley, Calif.: Institute of International Studies, 1981). Norwegian intelligence records of such incidents, however, report a much higher "background" rate than that, with the obvious conclusion that the number of such incidents reported in the press is not an accurate reflection of their frequency. Heradstveit indicates that during a period of concentrated attention such as this, the press nevertheless "overreports" incidents.

21. Leighton, "Soviet Strategy Towards Northern Europe and Japan," 129. Other aspects of Leighton's description of this event are somewhat dubious. Leighton also reports three other diverse incidents in April, May, and August 1983.

22. Carl Bildt, "Sweden and the Soviet Submarines," *Survival* 25, no. 4 (July–August 1983): 168.

23. "Hopes in Helsinki: Better Relations," *SvD*, November 27, 1985.

24. "No Finnish ASW," *DN*, May 10, 1983; Kaa Eneberg, "Foreign Minister Väyrynen: The Submarine Incidents Do Not Affect Finland," *DN*, May 20, 1983.

25. "Observations in the Gulf of Finland," *DN*, May 11, 1983.

26. "Hopes in Helsinki: Better Relations," *SvD*, November 27, 1985.

Chapter 3

1. Christer Larson, "Expensive Frugality: Good Submarine Warning System Scrapped in the 1970s," *Ny Teknik*, no. 22 (June 2, 1983): 7.

2. Hans Lindblad, "A Defense-Political Perspective," *The Sea of Peace*, Nils Andrén, ed. (Centralförbundet Folk och Försvar, 1982), 53–71. The motivation for the decision was developed in the government's 1970 defense analyses report, *Security and Defense Policy*, no. 4 (Stockholm: SOU, 1972): 206–207.

3. Roger Magnergård, "The Navy Had Help in the Search: Submarine's Fingerprint in Secret Swedish Archive," *SvD*, July 15, 1983.

4. C. Holmberg, "Naval Operations in Incidents – Theory and Practice," *Tidskrift För Sjöväsendet* (1970): 237–238. Warning munitions carried a charge of .5 kg., depth charges of 100 kg. Helicopters did not routinely carry depth charges and, therefore, nearly always used the warning munitions for warning purposes. Destroyers did the same, because the use of depth charges mandated a speed of 15 knots for the destroyer's safety, which risked the loss of sonar contact with the submarine.

5. "ASW by Helicopter," *MN*, no. 6 (1980): 67.

6. K. K. Hans von Hofsten, "The Government Must Speak Plainly: Naval Officer on the Government's Attitude on the Submarine Violations," *SvD*, November 3, 1985; Anders Öhman, "Armed ASW in the 1960s: Naval Officer Discloses Three Unknown Violations," *DN*, November 4, 1985.

7. Ibid.

8. K. K. Bror Stefenson, "Naval Expert: More Helicopters, Ships for Hunt for Submarine Spies," *DN*, September 19, 1969, reprinted in *MN*, no. 1 (1982): 2. In the early 1980s Stefenson was the chief of the defense staff during the period of the major incidents.

9. von Hofsten, "The Government Must Speak Plainly: Naval Officer on the Government's Attitude on the Submarine Violations."

10. "Time to Wake Up," *MN*, no. 6 (1981): 3. See also "ASW in the Baltic," *Vart Forsvar* 6, no. 6 (December 1980): 16–17. A press report described a strongly contradictory description as to how the submarine was first observed, claiming that it was detected by the dipping sonar of a helicopter about to begin monitoring the speed test of a new Swedish submarine. The Swedish submarine was ordered to surface, which caused a near-collision of the two submarines allegedly only "decimeters" from one another. This story does not, however, seem to be correct. Thorsten Engman, "Drama at Huvudskär: Soviet Submarine Close to Colliding with a Swedish One," *DN*, November 4, 1981.

11. Defense Staff Information Section, *Foreign Submarines in Swedish Territorial Waters*, no. 26 (October 2, 1980), Communiqué, mimeographed, 2 pages.

12. K. K. Hans von Hofsten, "Weapons Use Against Foreign Submarines," *MN*, no. 5 (1980): 2–3, 15.

13. von Hofsten, "The Government Must Speak Plainly: Na-

val Officer on the Government's Attitude on the Submarine Violations."

14. von Hofsten, "Weapons Use Against Foreign Submarines," 2–3, 15.

15. Defense Staff Information Section, *Incidents: 1980*, April 15, 1981, mimeographed, 11 pages.

16. Captain Hans Eihland, "Without Reconnaissance, No Knowledge," *MN*, no. 1 (1981): 12–13. The statement was made before a meeting of reserve officers in Karlskrona on April 26, 1980.

After the October 1980 events, the navy chief introduced the theme of the difficulty of ASW in the Baltic, noted that personnel had lost two weekends of free time during the operations, and noted that submarine violations were usually reported by the general public. Admiral Per Rydberg, "Astonishing Submarine Chase," *MN*, no. 5 (1980): 4.

17. Erik Krönmark, "We Must Get Sufficient Resources to Defend Our Neutrality," *MN*, no. 5 (1980): 3.

18. Ministry of Defense, *Sweden's Security Policy and Defense Planning: A Summary of an Interim Report by the 1978 Parliamentary Committee on Defense, February 1981*, no. 5 (Sweden: Ds Fö, 1981): 14, 17.

19. "New Method for ASW," *MN*, no. 3 (1981): 1. This event was also reported by Commander Lennart Forsman in *The Baltic: Yesterday – Today – Tomorrow*, 36; in the Moderate Party Report, *Countering the Submarine Threat*, 6; and in Åke Ortmark, "Major Deficiencies in Swedish Defense," *DN*, August 13, 1984.

20. Unless otherwise indicated, the 1981 events prior to October 1981 are taken from the Moderate Party Report, *Countering the Submarine Threat*, 5–6.

21. *Der Spiegel*, October 26, 1981.

22. Defense Staff Information Section, *Submarine 137 in Swedish Waters*, December 18, 1981, mimeographed, 14 pages.

23. Anders Hellberg and Anders Jorle, *Submarine 137, Ten Days that Shook Sweden* (Stockholm: Atlantis, 1984), 246–253, 260–264, 270–275.

24. "The Submarine Incident," Tass, November 7, 1981; reprint, *Soviet Weekly*, November 14, 1981.

25. These subsequent disclosures were made in the course of a debate that began in the Swedish public press on April 26,

1984 — the day that the Defense staff was to release its report of the March–April 1984 submarine intrusions in the same Karlskrona area. Three publicists contended that the earlier 1981 Whisky 137 (U-137) stranding had been a navigational accident. One, a well-known Swedish peace researcher, picking up a Soviet disinformation story released elsewhere in Europe, argued that drunkenness on board the Soviet submarine may have been a contributing cause to its navigational problems. The second and most persistent contention was by the journalist Ingemar Myrberg who published the book *Submarine Waltz* (Göteborg: Haga Bokförlag, 1985) for which Sweden's major peace organization awarded him a peace prize for "investigative journalism . . . and civil courage."

Both individuals had continued access to the special features and the guest editorial columns of Sweden's two major daily newspapers. The arguments were taken up by one of the editorial writers for *DN* (Sweden's major daily paper), who perpetuated the campaign. Myrberg's book not only claimed that the U-137 stranding was an accident but that all the other incidents reported by the Swedish navy, Defense staff, and government through 1985 were a total fabrication. This was at least a consistent argument, because there would be little sense in proving the Soviet case if one accepted that the Swedish allegations regarding all or most of the other submarine events spanning more than five years were valid. Finally, in November 1985, a strongly pro-Soviet filmmaker produced a film under public subsidy based on Myrberg's book that was shown on Swedish national television.

See various issues of *DN* and *SvD* from April 26, 1984 to July 1, 1984 and from November 19, 1985 to November 28, 1985. See also Hans Dahlberg, "Our Need to Be Deceived," *MN*, no. 8 (1984); 3.

26. Commander Lennart Forsman, "The Truth About U-137: Commander in Chief Releases Secret Material About the Soviet Submarine," *DN*, June 24, 1984; *MN*, no. 4 (1984): 16; Defense Staff Information Section, no title, December 2, 1985, mimeographed, 2 pages.

27. Lars Christiansson, "Intercepted Radio Message Evidence: Grounded U-137 Had Spy Mission," *SvD*, May 3, 1983; Sune Olofsson, "Submarine 137 Got Order to Blame Compass Error," *SvD*, June 25, 1984; *MN*, no. 4 (1984): 16.

28. Ministry of Foreign Affairs, "Soviet Submarine in Swed-

ish Archipelago," *Documents on Swedish Foreign Policy, 1981* (Stockholm: New Series, 1983): 81–101. See also *DN* and *SvD*, October 28, 1981 to November 10, 1981.

29. Hellberg and Jorle, *Submarine 137, Ten Days that Shook Sweden*, 253–255.

30. Ministry of Foreign Affairs, "Prime Minister Thorbjörn Fälldin, Opening Statement," Press Conference, November 5, 1981, mimeographed, 5 pages. See also Ministry of Foreign Affairs, *Documents on Swedish Foreign Policy, 1981*, pp. 81–101.

31. The official statement of the Swedish Defense Research Institute (FOA) reads as follows:

> In connection with the stranding of submarine 137, FOA has in consultation with the Defense staff, as a routine measure, carried out measurements of ionizing radiation from the submarine.
>
> Through such measurements it has been possible to establish that a quantity of uranium 238 is present in the bow of the submarine, presumably in a torpedo tube. This does not unambiguously prove that there is a nuclear warhead on board. We have, however, not found any other reasonable explanation for the presence of uranium 238. Our judgment is therefore that there is probably a nuclear warhead on board the submarine.

FOA Tidningen 19, no. 4 (December 1981): 2–9. Other possible uses for uranium 238 (U-238) in that location were apparently considered, assessed, and rejected by the agency.

32. Ministry of Foreign Affairs, "Prime Minister Thorbjörn Fälldin, Opening Statement," *Documents on Swedish Foreign Policy, 1981*, pp. 81–101.

33. Ibid.

34. Ibid.

35. Ibid.

36. "Soviet Government's Statement to the Government of Sweden," *Pravda*, November 12, 1981. Also as "Submarine: Swedish Statement Rejected," *Soviet Weekly* (November 21, 1981). See also Serge Schmemann, "Swedish Fears on Sub Dismissed by Moscow," *International Herald Tribune*, November 12, 1981.

The comment about international law has interesting implications in view of the North Korean capture of the USS *Pueblo* and the year-long trial of its crew in 1969 and in view of the USSR's habit in the postwar years of shooting down aircraft that crossed into its territorial airspace.

37. "Swedish Military: Systematic Disinformation from the USSR," *SvD*, July 28, 1985; Donald Fields, "Russia Turns Tables and Says Swedes Were Spying," *Guardian*, November 12, 1981. The Tass dispatch was given front-page exposure in the weekly newspaper *PAX*, published by Sweden's largest peace organization.

38. Colonel Daniel Proektor, interview, *DN*, November 10, 1981. One of the main points of the Tass dispatch was that everyone knew that U-238 was not used in nuclear weapons — only uranium 235 (U-235) and plutonium 239 (Pu-239). See Leonid Ponomaryov, "Much Ado . . . But What About," Tass, November 11, 1981.

The use of U-238 as a jacket, reflector, or "tamper" in nuclear warheads is nevertheless extensively described in a Soviet defense handbook published in 1958. See A. P. Glusijko, L. K. Markov, and L. P. Pilugin, *Nuclear Weapons and Nuclear Protection* (Moscow: Ministry of Defense, 1958); excerpts in *DN*, November 23, 1981. This official Soviet source claimed that up to 80 percent of the total energy released in thermonuclear detonation could be derived from such U-238 jacketing. Although the Soviet source is admittedly dated, a technical treatise on third-generation nuclear weapons published in 1985 describes the use of a beryllium and depleted U-238 tamper in modern second-generation weapons, as well as the use of an outer shell of U-238 in a modern fission-fusion-fission nuclear warhead. See Kosta Tsipis, "Third Generation Nuclear Weapons," *World Armaments and Disarmament, SIPRI Year Book 1985* (London: Taylor and Francis, 1985), 88–92.

The emissions from U-235 and Pu-239 cannot be detected through the thickness of metal of a submarine hull, while those of U-238 — or more specifically, those of some of its daughter products — can. U.S. naval officers indicated that they were not surprised by the reports and that "Soviet submarines usually put to sea with nuclear weapons aboard. . . . both the older Soviet submarines and the latest classes commonly carry nuclear weapons." See Richard Halloran, "Soviet Sub Threat Cited by U.S. Navy," *New York Times*, December 7, 1981.

39. "Soviet Sources to *Dagens Nyheter*, the Submarine is Utilized by Certain Forces," *DN*, December 23, 1981.

In November 1981, a month after the U-137 submarine stranding incident, Admiral of the Fleet Georgiy M. Jegoras, chief of the Soviet navy's main staff, was removed from his post. At the end of December, the head of the USSR's Northern Fleet, Admiral Vladimir Tschernavin, was also replaced. West German sources speculated that the two replacements in rapid succession were related to the stranding incident. This seems very unlikely, certainly regarding Admiral Tschernavin who was selected several years later to replace Admiral Gorshkov as head of the Soviet navy. See *Der Spiegel*, no. 4 (1982).

40. Erik Lidén and Roger Magnegård, "Commander in Chief's Report from 1981 on the U-137: Submarine in the Vicinity Many Days in Advance," *SvD*, November 22, 1985.

41. "Time to Wake Up," *MN*, 3.

42. Moderate Party Report, *Countering the Submarine Threat*, 67.

43. Defense Staff Information Section, "Submarine Violations," no. 211:31609, June 1, 1983, mimeographed, 12 pages. This unclassified report was apparently not released to the general public but was prepared to reach all personnel within the Swedish armed forces. The information it contains on identification of intruding submarines by acoustical recordings, electronic intercepts (radar emissions), and communications intercepts was not reproduced in the Report of the Submarine Defense Commission, though it must certainly have been presented to the commission, and it can be presumed to have been available to the press. An earlier summary of the events in Hårsfjärden released by the Defense staff (Defense Staff Information Section, "Submarine Activities in the Stockholm Southern Archipelago in October 1982," no. 911:32748, October 25, 1982, mimeographed, 8 pages) also did not contain this information. See also Mats Carlbom and Ingemar Löfgren, "Military's Secrets Indicate Submarines Were Soviet," *DN*, September 28, 1983. See also *DN* and *SvD* from September to October 1982.

44. "The Sound Was Decisive for Us," *DN*, May 15, 1984. The point concerning the precise keel measurements did not appear in the commission's report either, but was released through interviews by the chief of the Defense staff later in 1983 and 1984.

45. UK Ministry of Defense, "A Selection of Soviet Submersibles," *Recognition Journal*, no. 9 (1985); reprint, *MN*, no. 1 (1986): 8–9.

46. Anders Ohman, "Naval Staff's Pictures: Here Are the USSR's Midget Submarines," *DN*, March 7, 1986.

47. *Morskoi Sbornik*, no. 6 (1985): 86–90.

48. Submarine Defense Commission, *Countering the Submarine Threat: Submarine Violations and Swedish Security Policy*, no. 13 (Stockholm: SOU, 1983).

49. Ibid., 79–80.

50. Ibid., 80.

51. Ibid., 42, 49, 81.

52. Ibid., 41. Anders Hasselbom, a Swedish journalist for the newspaper *Dagens Industri* (*Daily Industry*), claimed during the Hårsfjärden ASW operations that it was a NATO submarine that was being chased by the Swedish navy. He also subsequently wrote a book to the same effect, which accused the Swedish military of misleading the commission and the commission of misleading the public. See Anders Hasselbom, *Submarine Threat* (Stockholm: Prisma, 1984). See also "To Counter Submarine Allegations," *DN*, May 15, 1984; Harald Hamrin, "New Book Criticizes Submarine Commission: A NATO Submarine Was in Hårsfjärden," *DN*, May 15, 1984.

53. Bildt, "Sweden and the Soviet Submarines," 165–169. See also Lieutenant General Stig Löfgren, "Soviet Submarines Against Swedes," *Strategic Review* 12, no. 1 (Winter 1984); 36–42.

54. Carl Bildt, "Submarine Defense Commission's Conclusions Remain Binding," *SvD*, October 2, 1985.

55. See occasional articles in *MN* from 1981 through 1986.

56. Carl Bildt, "The Future of Northern Europe," in *Northern Europe: Security Issues for the 1990s*, Paul M. Cole and Douglas M. Hart, eds. (Boulder, Colo.: Westview Press, 1986), 123–151.

57. Submarine Defense Commission, *Countering the Submarine Threat: Submarine Violations and Swedish Security Policy*, 53.

58. Olle Rossander, "Mines Are Effective Weapons," *DN*, May 6, 1983.

59. Submarine Defense Commission, *Countering the Submarine Threat: Submarine Violations and Swedish Security Policy*, 57.

60. Ibid., 55–56.

61. Ibid., 44–45. These rumors were again repeated in 1986 by the British expert on Soviet military organization, John Erickson. See Bengt Lindström and Ingemar Löfgren, "British Re-

searcher on the Submarine Hunt in Hårsfjärden: Sweden Capitu-
lated to the USSR," *DN*, January 13, 1986.

62. "Swedish note," *DN*, April 4, 1983.

63. Swedish Prime Minister Olof Palme, Press Conference
Statement, April 26, 1983.

64. Elisabeth Crona, "Palme Warns of Worsened Relations:
Trust of the USSR Shaken," *SvD*, April 27, 1983; Åke Ekdahl,
"Sharp Protest Against Submarine Violations: Palme Warns
Against New Attempts," *DN*, April 27, 1983.

65. R. W. Apple, Jr., "Sweden Hands Russia Stiff Protest on
Subs: Palme Warns Intruders Will Be Sunk," *International Herald
Tribune*, April 27, 1983.

66. *DN*, May 9, 1984; *Expressen*, May 8, 1984.

67. Fredrik Braconier and Lars Christiansson, *Who Guards
Sweden?* (Stockholm: Timbro Förlag, 1985), 162. This book contains the best available record of the Ferm, Arbatov, and the
related affairs discussed below. See particularly pages 161 to
166.

68. "'Admit It,' I've Often Said to Soviets," *SvD*, September
29, 1985.

69. The description given here is not taken from press accounts. It is based on personal interviews I made on May 16, 1983
with three of the participants at the seminar. For press accounts
see *DN*, May 15, 1983, and *SvD*, May 17, 1983.

70. Sven Svensson, "Palme on the Arbatov Affair: An Expression of the Arrogance of Power," *DN*, May 21, 1983.

71. "Arbatov Denies Provocation," *DN*, May 24, 1983.

72. Lars Christiansson, "No Nationality Determined at
Hårsfjärden: New Statement by Arbatov on Foreign Submarines,"
SvD, July 20, 1983.

73. "Olof Palme – A Controversial Person," TV-2, 8 P.M.,
March 14, 1986.

74. See *DN*, May 21 and 22, 1983. Bildt is somewhat of an
anomaly in Swedish parliamentary politics. He is one of probably
only two members of the entire parliament who is competently
informed about weapon and defense issues.

75. The full text of the Parliamentary Constitutional Committee questioning of Prime Minister Palme, Ambassador Anders
Ferm, and Carl Bildt subsequently appeared in print. See *Tempus*, May 16, 1984, pp. 6–11.

76. Braconier and Christiansson, *Who Guards Sweden?* 163.

77. Defense Staff Information Section, *Submarine Incidents, Summer 1983*, September 16, 1983, mimeographed, 12 pages.

78. Defense Staff Information Section, *Compilation, Submarine Violations, Fall 1983*, December 20, 1983, mimeographed, 5 pages; and *Diver Activities in the Stockholm Archipelago, September 1983*, May 9, 1984, mimeographed, 9 pages; Lars Christiansson and Roger Magnergård, "Defense Suspects Entry by Foreign Divers: 'No Accident That Mines Disappeared,'" *SvD*, August 3, 1985; Roger Magnergård, "Navy Chief: Submarines Continue to Violate," *SvD*, November 17, 1983.

79. *Statement by the Minister of Defense Anders Thunborg Concerning the Supreme Commander's Report on the Submarine Incidents in the Summer of 1983*, mimeographed, 3 pages; Sven Svensson, "Since Hårsfjärden: No Further Submarines Have Been Identified," *DN*, September 14, 1985; Kenneth Ahlborn, "Carl Bildt, Submarine Commission: Controversial Evidence Not in the Report," *DN*, September 12, 1983; "Bildt Wants to Identify the USSR Midget Submarines Says the Commander in Chief," *DN*, September 17, 1983. The government was aided in maintaining this essentially untenable position by the professional and technical incompetence of the Swedish media and apparent naiveté of large sectors of its political elite and public.

80. The note was printed in full in *DN* on May 7, 1983. Whereas in 1981 the official Swedish annual compilation of government documents on important foreign policy matters had included the USSR's rejection of the Swedish protest note on the U-137 submarine stranding, the 1983 edition of this same annual compilation (now during the Social Democratic government) omitted the USSR's note of rejection of the second Swedish protest note relating to the Hårsfjärden events.

81. *Izvestia*, June 3, 1983; "Who Benefits," *Izvestia*, May 15, 1983.

82. Sven Svensson, "Soviets Wanted to Participate in the Submarine Investigation: Joint Rejection by All Parties," *DN*, December 13, 1983.

83. "A Public Secret," *SvD*, May 7, 1984. The additional material was delivered to the USSR between August and September of 1983. This would appear to be a case in which secrecy was unquestionably used to withhold information, not from an antagonist, but from the public.

84. *MN*, no. 5–6 (December 1982): 4–5.

85. Y. Konenkov, "A Faked-Up Press Report That Got Drowned in the Baltic," *Komsomolskaya Pravda*, February 6, 1983. See also *Novoje Vremja*, June 3, 1983.

86. "Who Benefits," *Izvestia*, May 15, 1983.

87. Igor Pavlov, "Written in the Water," Novosti Press Agency, June 3, 1983.

88. "Once More About the Submarine," *Izvestia*, March 18, 1983.

89. Tass, May 7, 1983.

90. Ibid., April 27, 1983. See also May 8, 1983.

91. Ivan Amblomov, Ibid., April 29, 1983.

92. Lars Christiansson, "Palme Received Reply: Andropov Message from Koivisto," *SvD*, February 29, 1984.

93. Lars Christiansson, "We Respect Your Territory: Sweden gets New Soviet Assurance," *SvD*, March 13, 1984.

94. "Foreign Minister Bodström: Increase Exchanges with the USSR," *DN*, January 4, 1984.

95. "Gromyko Promises Palme: No Intrusion in Swedish Waters," *DN*, January 17, 1984.

96. Thorwald Olsson, "Ola Ullsten on Submarine Traffic: Gromyko Has Promised Before," *DN*, January 18, 1984.

97. Sven Svensson, "New Soviet Assurance: Your Neutrality is Respected," *DN*, January 19, 1984.

98. Lars Christiansson, "Bodström on Swedish Security Policy: Soviet's Only Intention Friendship with Sweden," *SvD*, April 1, 1980.

99. Harald Hamrin, "Gromyko to Palme: Stop Talking About Submarines," *DN*, April 5, 1986. See also *DN* and *SvD* for April 6 and 7, 1986.

100. "Palme After *DN*'s Disclosures: The Picture is Incomplete," *DN*, April 7, 1984. See also *DN*, April 11, 1984.

101. Harald Hamrin, "Palme on the Superpowers and Sweden: Even Our Borders are Holy," *DN*, October 9, 1983. See also editorial.

102. Defense Staff Information Section, *The Submarine Incident in Karlskrona, Spring 1984*, May 7, 1984, mimeographed, 10 pages; Commander in Chief's Report, *ASW Submarine Defense Activities in the Karlskrona Area During February–April 1984*, May 3, 1984, Op. 2, 763:31550, mimeographed, 124 pages. See also *DN* and *SvD*, February 10, 1984 to April 1, 1985.

103. Defense Staff Information Section, *The Submarine Inci-*

dent in Karlskrona, Spring 1984, 1; Commander in Chief's Report, *ASW Submarine Defense Activities in the Karlskrona Area During February–April 1984,* p. 12.

104. Defense Staff Information Section, *The Submarine Incident in Karlskrona, Spring 1984,* 6.

105. Vice Admiral Bengt Schuback, "Head of the Navy on Submarine Violations and Defense Resources: 'Efforts Haven't Been Sufficient,'" *SvD,* November 8, 1985.

106. Roger Magnergård, "Future Head of the Navy: 'New Weapons Will Stop Submarines,'" *SvD,* May 6, 1984.

107. Lars Christiansson, "Vice Admiral Bror Stefenson Confirms New Bottom Tracks from Midget Submarine, 'We Reacted Too Slowly in Karlskrona,'" *DN,* July 29, 1985.

108. Sven Svensson, "Commander in Chief's Report on Submarine Defenses: Naval Bases Will Get Fixed Barriers," *DN,* October 25, 1984; Sven Svensson, "Permanent Barriers at Bases," *DN,* October 27, 1984.

109. "Violations Can Be Introduced," *DN,* May 11, 1984.

110. Hamrin, "Palme on the Superpowers and Sweden: Even Our Borders Are Holy." "The responsible political leadership must be extremely precise in its statements. I must operate on the assumption that it cannot be said with certainty that there have been violations and that we cannot establish the identity of them."

111. Carl Bildt, "Violated – or Not Violated," *SvD,* April 3, 1984. The single newspaper reference was in an editorial in the Social Democratic morning paper *Stockholms-Tidningen,* whose managing editor had a strong interest in security issues.

112. Defense Staff Information Section, *Incidents During the Second and Third Quarter 1984,* no. 911:33828, October 26, 1984, mimeographed, 5 pages; and *Incidents During the Fourth Quarter 1984 Together with a Brief Summary of the Incidents for All of 1984,* January 31, 1985, mimeographed, 8 pages. See also *DN,* August 19 and October 27, 1984 and *SvD,* October 27, 1984 and January 31, 1985.

113. Roger Magnergård, "We Aren't Saying Where," *SvD,* October 27, 1984.

114. Schuback, "Head of the Navy on Submarine Violations and Defense Resources: 'Efforts Haven't Been Sufficient.'" There was at least one contrary suggestion with regard to the reporting of the 1984 Karlskrona events. See Björn Höijes, "Dissatisfaction

Among the Military: Not Allowed to Inform as Much About Submarines as They Wished to," *Tempus*, April 14, 1984.

115. See *DN*, August 25 and 26, September 5, 6, 8, and 10, October 21 and 22, 1984; *SvD*, August 25 and 26, September 1, 5–7, 12, and 15, October 13 and 22, 1984.

A Suchoi-15 is the same type of Soviet interceptor that shot down the Korean airliner in 1984. Swedish military radar controllers did not inform the Scanair pilots that they were being intercepted.

116. Defense Staff Information Section, *Soviet Aircraft Violation*, September 7, 1984, mimeographed, 3 pages.

117. Harald Hamrin, "Senior Soviet Official Shows *DN* Secret Map: Our Aircraft Never Violated Swedish Territory," *DN*, October 21, 1984.

118. Harald Hamrin, "Sweden Uninformed," *DN*, October 21, 1984.

119. See *SvD*, September 3–9, 1985.

120. See *SvD* and *DN*, September 20, 1985. On January 2, 1986, the Norwegian Defense Ministry announced that a Soviet cruise missile fired from a Soviet ship in the Barents Sea on December 28, 1985 had crossed Norwegian territory and landed in Finland. At no point in the days that followed did Finnish authorities identify the USSR as the responsible party. The Finnish authorities referred only to an "unidentified flying object" that entered Finnish airspace.

The missile was an older generation SSN-3 Shaddock cruise missile and had been launched from a Soviet Juliet or Echo-II-class submarine during a naval exercise. The Soviet navy test fires cruise missiles regularly in the Barents Sea to familiarize submarine crews with the weapons, and the missile may additionally have been intended to pass over portions of the Soviet Kola Peninsula for possible use as a surface-to-air missile target or in air defense readiness exercises. Guidance on the missile presumably malfunctioned, and it crossed over a small portion of Norwegian territory to land in Finland.

On other occasions, the USSR has also carried out missile tests in international waters in the Barents Sea with the target area lying in the disputed western portion of an area under contention with Norway. In another category of submarine missile tests, Soviet ballistic missile submarines on their way back to bases in the Kola Peninsula after a tour of duty in the Atlantic often launch a missile from positions about 100 miles northwest of Norway's Lofoten Islands. The missiles' target area is within the land area of the USSR.

Norway filed a protest on January 4, 1986 and two hours after the Finnish government requested an investigation, the USSR offered an explanation and an apology to both Finland and Norway. The USSR stated that "a flying target had gone off-course during exercises in the Barents Sea," and that "it could not be excluded that it flew partly over Norwegian territory and then into Finnish territory." The primary reason for the Soviet apology was presumed to be that the missile had landed on Finnish soil and its parts would eventually be found and identified. In fact, this occurred within a month, and Finland returned the portions that were found to the USSR at the Soviet request.

See *DN* and *SvD*, January 3–6, 1985; "Flight Trajectory of the SSN-3," *International Defense Review* 18, no. 2 (February 1985): 140; "Finns Scour Lake for Missile: Oslo Plans Protest but Says Cruise Malfunctioned," *Washington Post*, January 4, 1985; Olav Trygge Starvik, "From Submarines Off Lofoten: Soviet Rocket Tests Near Norway," *Aftenposten*, January 13 and 16, 1986; "Debris Shows Soviet Rocket Was Not a Cruise Missile," *Washington Post*, February 3, 1985; *DN* and *SvD*, January 31, 1985 to February 6, 1985.

121. Örjan Berner, *The USSR and the Nordic States: Cooperation, Security, and Conflicts During Fifty Years* (Stockholm: Bonnier, 1985), 70–73. On July 7, 1985, a Soviet Suchoi-15 aircraft trailing a Swedish reconnaissance Viggen during Soviet maneuvers in international waters in the southeastern Baltic crashed into the sea.

122. Cable to Swedish Foreign Minister Lennart Bodström from USSR Ministry of Foreign Affairs, Moscow, March 15, 1984.

123. Y. Kuznetsov, "USSR-Sweden: Good Neighborly Relations to Mutual Advantage," *Pravda*, March 15, 1984.

124. "The Soviet Union Consistently Strives for Good Neighborly Relations with Sweden," *Novosti Press Agency*, August 2, 1985.

125. Mikael Rosquist, "Submarines Discussed Via Diplomatic Channels," *Tempus*, March 27, 1984. The parliamentary trip was to have taken place in the early fall and eventually fell through, not because of the Karlskrona submarine violations but

because of the Soviet interceptor and Swedish airliner incident in the summer. Following this, two of the non-Socialist parties declared their disinterest in participating in the proposed visit.

126. Alexander Bovin, "*Izvestia* on Swedish-Soviet Relations: Who Benefits by the Constant Chill," *DN*, March 27, 1984.

127. Nikolaj Jefimov, "More Antagonistic than the Press in NATO Countries," *SvD*, February 14, 1984; Stefan Teste, "Soviet Demands Met by the Conformity of Silence: Why Does Olof Palme Keep Silent?" *DN*, April 27, 1984.

128. Alexander Sytchev, "In Our Common Interest," *SvD*, August 4, 1985. Later in 1984, the Soviet ambassador formally protested to the Swedish Ministry of Foreign Affairs about the publication in Sweden of a book on Soviet industrial espionage in Sweden. See *DN* and *SvD*, October 23–27 and November 7–9, 1984.

This study does not discuss two other issues that produced press commentary strongly critical of the USSR in both Norway and Sweden between November 1983 and February 1984. Those issues centered on the disclosure that a member of the Norwegian Foreign Ministry had been spying for the USSR for more than a decade and on the disclosure of a major computer and data smuggling operation to the USSR that involved a Swedish importer as an intermediary.

129. "Submarine Hallucinations," *Krasnaya Zvezda*, February 28, 1984.

130. N. Svanov, "No Fun," *Izvestia*, March 3, 1984. See also the "comic" pieces "Dope from Abroad," which referred to "the slow-witted Swedes," by O. Vakulovski in *Sovetskaya Rossia*, February 24, 1984, and "They Have Caught It at Last," *Izvestia*, April 28, 1984.

131. E. Kovalev, "Nothing to Show," *Izvestia*, April 12, 1984.

132. *Pravda*, April 15, 1984, quoted in *Tempus*, April 17, 1984, p. 2.

133. Koivisto reportedly later claimed that he had actually not seen the commission's report. On a third occasion Koivisto apparently said that the Hårsfjärden evidence was unsatisfactory — it was just "ghosts."

Kaa Eneberg, "Koivisto Distrusts Submarine Commission's Report: Still Much to Clarify," *DN*, May 19, 1983; "Koivisto's Thoughts," *DN*, May 21, 1983; Jan-Anders Ekström, "Koivisto on Soviet Submarine Violations: Much is Still Unclear," *SvD*, May

19, 1983; Lars Christiansson, "Statement a Misunderstanding," *SvD*, May 19, 1983.

134. Jan-Anders Ekström, "Koivisto on Sweden: The Submarines are Fantasies," *SvD*, December 20, 1984.

135. Harald Hamrin, "Palme-Koivisto: No Joint Statement," *DN*, January 6, 1985.

136. "Discussions with Palme Cleared the Air: Koivisto Doesn't Doubt Soviets' Submarine Violations," *DN*, January 8, 1985.

137. Harald Hamrin, "Bodström Doubts Submarine Allegations: Hysteria Surrounds Violations," *DN*, February 3, 1985. Six journalists had been present at the session. Five could subsequently reconstruct the conversation from their notes and a tape recording. The sixth supported the foreign minister in disclaiming the report. See *DN* and *SvD*, February 3-7, 1985.

138. "Fälldin Following the Statements: Bodström Should Resign," *DN*, February 4, 1985.

139. "The Guardian of Authority," *DN*, March 31, 1985. See also "Palme Continues the Conflict," *DN*, March 28, 1985; Magdalena Ribbing, "All the Bridges Broken to the Final Bastion," *DN*, March 28, 1985.

140. Sven Svensson, "Palme Warns: Conservatives' Tactics Playing with Fire," *DN*, April 16, 1985; Åke Ekdahl, "Bodström: The Conservatives Are a Factor of Risk," *DN*, April 16, 1985.

141. Fredrik Braconier, "Is Andersson's Flying Start Sufficient?" *SvD*, October 17, 1985.

142. Defense Staff Information Section, *Particular Information Regarding Underwater Activities*, October 17, 1985, mimeographed, 7 pages. The first three quarterly reports for 1985 were issued by the Defense Staff Information Section on April 29, July 8, and October 17, 1985. References to the other events referred to appeared in *DN*, April 12, 1985, and *SvD*, April 12-13, June 28, July 3, 9, 11, August 26, and October 6, 1985; Swedish Television, News Report, Channel 2, 7 P.M., March 28, 1985.

143. Secretary of State Pierre Schori reported that "he had taken the temperature" of the relations "and found them normal." See *SvD* and *DN*, August 7, 8, 1985. Schori was also quoted as saying either that the Soviet minister "had expressed his respect for Swedish neutrality being as hard as rock," or "that the Soviet minister's respect for Swedish neutrality was as hard as rock." Both versions appeared in *SvD*, August 8, 1985.

144. Telegraphens Telegrambureau interview with General Bengt Gustafsson, July 21, 1985, teletype text. Also in "Commander Bengt Gustafsson: Too Small Resources Go to Defense," *SvD*, July 22, 1985.

145. Defense Staff Information Section, *Information Regarding Submarine Violations*, Communiqué no. 12, July 22, 1985. Also in "Defense Staff Retreats: Denies Gustafsson's Statement," *DN*, July 23, 1985.

146. Lars Christiansson, "No Evidence that Soviet Is Responsible for the Violations," *SvD*, July 23, 1985.

147. Defense Staff Information Section, *Incidents During the Fourth Quarter 1985 and Short Summary for All of 1985*, January 24, 1986, mimeographed, 7 pages. See also *SvD* and *DN*, January 25, 1986.

148. Bengt Falkkloo, "Hydrophone Recordings Made: Defense Staff Keeps Silent About Submarine," *DN*, January 21, 1986; Roger Magnergård, "Commander in Chief's Report on the Fourth Quarter: Many Submarine Sounds Recorded," *SvD*, January 20, 1986; Lars Christiansson, "Vessels Probably from the East," *SvD*, January 20, 1986.

149. Defense Staff Information Section, *Special Information Regarding National Identification During Submarine Defense Activities*, January 24, 1986, mimeographed, 5 pages.

150. Christiansson, "Vessels Probably from the East."

151. "New Signs of Violations," *DN*, January 25, 1986.

152. Erik Lidén, "Questioning an Overreaction," *SvD*, October 25, 1985.

153. "Commander in Chief on Submarine Incidents: Government Informed," *SvD*, November 5, 1985; "Commander in Chief Disputes Palme," *SvD*, October 18, 1985; "Reality the Worst Enemy," *SvD*, November 7, 1985.

154. Roger Magnergård, "The *Iowa* Rumbles in the Sea of Peace," *SvD*, October 19, 1985.

155. Lars Christiansson and Roger Magnergård, "The Navy Can Only Defend a Limited Portion of the Coast," *SvD*, November 5, 1985; Schuback, "Head of Navy on Submarine Violations and Defense Resources: 'Efforts Haven't Been Sufficient'"; Braconier, "Is Andersson's Flying Start Sufficient?"

156. Lars Christiansson, "Twelve Naval Officers Support von Hofsten: The Government Doesn't Take the Submarine Threat and Violations Seriously," *SvD*, November 10, 1985.

157. Åke Ekdahl and Sven Svensson, "Olof Palme Rebuts Naval Officers' Criticism: Injudicious and Incorrect," *DN*, November 12, 1985. See also *DN*, November 11, 14, and 30, 1985; Lars Christiansson, "Defense Minister on the Officers' Criticisms: Unreasonable Insinuations," *SvD*, November 12, 1985. See also *SvD*, November 13, 1985.

158. Statement by Swedish Prime Minister Olof Palme on October 21, 1985 on the occasion of the commemoration of the fortieth anniversary of the United Nations.

159. Nils Sköld, "We Must Be Prepared for Surprise Attack!" *MN*, no. 1 (1981): 3. Late in 1980, then Defense Minister Erik Krönmark had also drawn attention to surprise attack and in a context directly related to the first major ASW operation. See page 12; Krönmark, "We Must Get Sufficient Resources to Defend Our Neutrality," 3.

160. Viktor Suvorov, "Spetsnaz, the Soviet Union's Special Forces," *International Defense Review*, no. 9 (September 1983): 1209–1216; Viktor Suvorov, "Soviet Special Forces at Work in the Baltic," *Jane's Naval Review*, John Moore, ed. (London: Jane's Publishing Company, 1985), 142–149.

161. Major Håkan Swedin, "Sabotage Units," *Arme Nytt*, no. 2 (1985): 24–25; *Arme Nytt*, no. 3 (1985): 23.

162. Lars Christiansson and Roger Magnergård, "Threaten Sweden," *SvD*, July 28, 1985; "Picture Selling Cover for Spying," *SvD*, August 5, 1985. See also also *SvD*, December 13, 1985, January 18, 19, 21, and 23, 1986; *DN*, January 29, 1986.

163. Anita Sjöblom, "Elite Units Trained as Defense Against Sabotage," *DN*, January 22, 1986.

164. Address of Swedish Prime Minister Olof Palme on Swedish security policy, Swedish Institute of International Affairs, December 12, 1985.

165. Lars Christiansson, "Gunnar Nilsson Resigns Unexpectedly," *SvD*, January 10, 1986; Carl Bildt, "Change of Chairman," *SvD*, January 13, 1986.

166. There was one Swedish-Soviet naval incident in 1985 not related to the submarine violations. The incident was of the type that occurs more commonly between U.S. and other NATO and Soviet vessels on the high seas. A Swedish electronic intercept vessel was observing the trials of a new Soviet Kilo-class submarine in international waters in the Baltic. It approached the submarine on the surface and, in the subsequent efforts by an

accompanying Soviet surface escort to get the Swedish boat to leave the area, the Soviet vessel scraped the Swedish one slightly. "First Kilo Submarine in the Baltic," *SvD*, November 1, 1985. See *DN*, October 30, 31, 1985, November 1, 9, 1985; *SvD*, October 30, 31, 1985, November 1, 3, 4, 7, and 9, 1985.

167. E. Potapov, "Hackneyed Myth Relaunched," *Izvestia*, May 14, 1985.

168. P. Kononov, "Northern Europe in Washington's Distorting Mirror," *Izvestia*, June 14, 1985. See also Y. Kuznetsov, "Bundesmarine: How Far Can It Go," *Pravda*, July 4, 1984; M. Kostikov, "There Is No Stopping NATO," *Pravda*, July 5, 1984; Y. Kuznetsov, "Vindictive Pressure," *Pravda*, November 21, 1985; A. Sychov, "Old Hat from U.S. Ambassador," *Izvestia*, February 4, 1986.

169. Kaa Eneberg, "Carlsson After Soviet Trip: Friendly and Stable Relations," *DN*, April 18, 1986.

170. Defense Staff Information Section, *Incidents During the Third Quarter 1986*, October 20, 1986, mimeographed, 4 pages; Åke Ekedahl, "New Report on Submarine Violations: Earlier Pattern Continues," *DN*, October 17, 1986; Anders Öhman, "Defense Staff: Suspected Submarine Seen Among 15 New Cases," *DN*, October 21, 1986. The number "15" does not appear in the Defense staff report itself, but in the news stories that accompanied it. The number was obviously leaked to the press. The report also makes no mention of technical indications that were obtained by various Swedish ships in ASW operations during the summer.

171. Anders Jonsson and Roger Magnergård, "Fifteen Certain Violations," *SvD*, October 18, 1986.

172. Lars Christiansson, "Sverker Åström: Violating Submarines Are Soviet," *SvD*, October 11, 1986.

173. Sven Svensson, "No Submarines, Koivisto Maintains," *DN*, October 22, 1986. Soviet Lieutenant General Nikolai Chervov has described this incident with a crucial difference. On a visit to Stockholm in October 1986, Chervov disclosed that he and Soviet Defense Minister Sergey Sokolov visited Helsinki in the fall of 1985. During a visit with Koivisto and the Finnish defense minister, the defense minister introduced the subject by saying, "*We* have indications of submarines in *our* waters. Should we attack them?" [Emphasis added.] Sokolov replied, "You are welcome, go ahead and bomb. Use bombs, then everyone will see

that the submarines are not Soviet." Sweden TV-1 news, October 26, 1986. Chervov repeated this in answer to a question following his address at the military academy in Stockholm.

174. Harald Hamrin, "Ingvar Carlsson in *Pravda* Interview: Clear Emphasis Against Submarine Violations," *DN*, October 28, 1986. The segment on Swedish-Soviet relations was omitted from the version of the interview distributed by Tass.

175. Anders Öhman, "Four Violations by the Warsaw Pact," *DN*, November 12, 1986.

176. Vice Admiral Bengt Schuback, "Head of the Navy on the Quality and Quantity of Submarine Defense: Still No Deterrent Effect on Foreign Submarines," *SvD*, November 10, 1986. Emil Svensson, "Our Signals Are Incorrect," *DN*, November 21, 1986.

Chapter 4

1. At least one commentator suggested that the situation forced the USSR to continue the incursions rather that stop them because the USSR denied responsibility for the events. Following this logic, the Soviets would have demonstrated their responsibility if the events had stopped after a Swedish protest. (Although this is plausible, a third party also could have stopped due to increased risk in the face of Swedish ASW operations.) See Commander Åke Johnson, "Soviet Units," *SvD*, January 31, 1984.

2. Braconier, "Confrontation at Hårsfjärden: Credulity Versus Grim Reality."

3. Åke Ortmark, "Major Shortcomings in Swedish Defense," *DN*, August 13, 1984.

4. There is no reason to believe that Swedish authorities avoided more direct attacks at the submarines because of the possibility that the intruding submarines all carried nuclear weapons, as was discovered in the case of the U-137. This would, at the most, have resulted in some degree of plutonium contamination if a weapon had been directly ruptured. None of the intruding submarines were nuclear-powered.

5. "Submarines and Superpower Threat," *DN*, March 3, 1986.

6. "Relations with the USSR Have Improved," *SvD*, November 25, 1985.

7. The 1984 Defense Committee, *Sweden's Security Policy: Entering the 90s*, no. 23 (Stockholm: SOU, 1985), 44.

8. See "Soviet Violations," *SvD*, January 20, 1986; "Submarine Debate Without Palme," *DN*, December 17, 1985; "Sten Anderson on the Wrong Track," *SvD*, November 25, 1985.

9. Lars Christiansson, "Expectations in Helsinki: Better Relations Between Stockholm and Moscow," *SvD*, November 27, 1985.

10. Harald Hamrin, "Submarine Violations 'Temporary': Appeal to Sweden to Show Consideration," *DN*, April 11, 1984.

11. Sven Svensson, "Soviet Distrusts Swedish Neutrality," *DN*, May 22, 1983.

12. Lars Christiansson, "Finland's Foreign Minister: Submarine Violations Have Not Changed the Nordic Situation," *SvD*, June 10, 1984; Kaa Eneberg, "Foreign Minister Varynen: The Submarine Affairs Don't Affect Finland," *DN*, May 20, 1983.

13. Christiansson, "Expectations in Helsinki: Better Relations Between Stockholm and Moscow."

14. Svante Nycander, "With Fingers in the Jam Jar," *DN*, October 23, 1985. Retired British Vice Admiral Sir Ian McGeoch, an ex-submarine commander, was responsible for his contributions in a British TV appearance and newspaper article, "Sweden Suffers from Periscope Sickness," *Aftonbladet*, February 20, 1984. Rebuttal by Admiral Bror Stefensson, "The Admiral Has a Bad Memory," *Aftonbladet*, May 20, 1984.

15. "Submarines a Bluff by the Defense Forces," *DN*, May 8, 1983.

16. Anders Thunborg, "Our Neutrality is Respected in the World Around Us," *Folk och Försvar* 13, no. 1 (March 1983): 4–5.

17. Anders Thunborg, "Security Policy No Place for Daydreams," *SvD*, February 8, 1986.

18. Olle Svensson, "Submarine Debate Was Useful," *DN*, December 20, 1985.

19. "Security – A Defense Issue," *DN*, January 4, 1986.

20. Ortmark, "Major Shortcomings in Swedish Defense."

21. Thunborg, "Security Policy No Place for Daydreams."

22. Sven Svensson, "Midget Submarines Special Weapon for Scandinavia: Sweden Must Soon Escalate the Hunt," *DN*, September 25, 1983.

23. This and the quotation that follows both appeared in Andres Kung and Jorgen Weibull, "Security Situation Nothing to

Joke About," *SvD*, November 12, 1985. In November 1985 the newly appointed foreign minister took up the Soviet propagated theme of "the responsibility of journalists" for Swedish security and independence. "Response to Sten Andersson's Criticism: Resembles an Attempt to Stifle the Press," *SvD*, November 3, 1985.

24. "Anders Thunborg at the Party Congress: The Demands of Reality Will Determine the Balance," *MN*, no. 5 (1984): 6–7.

25. Defense Staff Information Section, *Submarine Incidents, Summer 1983*, p. 6. In 1985–1986 exchange rates, 600 million crowns was equivalent to $86 million.

26. "Submarine Debate Without Palme," *DN*, December 17, 1985.

27. Erik Lidén, "Roine Carlsson: Air Force and Air Defense Must Be Given Priority," *SvD*, January 30, 1986. For other sources on defense budgeting decisions regarding the Swedish navy see Defense Staff Information Section, *Commander in Chief's Submarine Defense Plan*, no. 911:33829, October 26, 1984, mimeographed, 8 pages; *OB 85: Perpective Plan, Part II*, October 1, 1985.

28. "Interview: Olof Palme, 'Europe is in a State of Insecurity,'" *Newsweek*, October 24, 1983, p. 56.

29. Harald Hamrin, "New Information on the Violations: Midget Submarines Were Already Here in the 1970s," *DN*, February 1, 1985.

30. Lars Christiansson, "Soviet Politburo Responsible for the Violations," *SvD*, February 14, 1985.

31. At times such comments in a more serious diplomatic vein also were published in the Soviet press. For example "USSR-Sweden: Good Neighborly Relations to Mutual Advantage," *Pravda*, March 15, 1984.

32. Ilja Baranikas, "Good Neighborly Relations: Sweden-Soviet Union," *SvD*, April 1981.

33. Harald Hamrin, "Soviet Criticizes the Commander in Chief," *DN*, September 5, 1983; Harald Hamrin, "Soviet Criticism of Swedish-U.S. Cooperation: Neutrality Has Been Damaged," *DN*, October 8, 1983. It was also Zagladin who showed Hamrin the contrived map of Soviet aircraft locations in October 1984 following the Soviet rejection of Swedish protests of the air incursion incident. In this case and the two below, the USSR was afforded the opportunity to reach Sweden directly with its mes-

sage through a Swedish correspondent who traveled to Moscow for interviews.

34. Harald Hamrin, "Russian Top Military: Sweden Lies About Submarine Tracks," *DN*, October 1, 1983.

35. Harald Hamrin, "Report from Moscow: Swedish Policies Met with Suspicion," *DN*, October 26, 1984.

36. Lev Voronkov, *Non-Nuclear Status to Northern Europe* (Moscow: Nauka Publishers, 1984).

37. Juri Denisov, "Soviet Invitation to Industrial Collaboration," *DN*, January 7, 1986. When Viktor Tjebrikov announced a minute of silence at the USSR's 27th Party Congress in honor of Olof Palme, he stated, "We will never forget how much Olof Palme did to develop good neighborly relations between his country and the Soviet Union." "Arbatov: 'Personal Loss,'" *Dagens Industri: Memory of Palme*, March 3, 1986, p. 6.

38. Milton Leitenberg, "The Stranded USSR Submarine in Sweden and the Question of a Nordic Nuclear-Free Zone," *Cooperation and Conflict*, no. 17 (1982): 17–18.

39. Estimates made by the author in 1980 on the assumption that *all* available shipborne cruise missile launchers were nuclear-armed, and not accounting for the possibility of reloads, are as follows:

> Cruise and ballistic missiles in the Baltic 102
> Cruise and ballistic missiles in the Northern Fleet . 916
> Nuclear torpedoes (assuming 1–2 per
>   submarine). . . . . 281 or 562
> Land-based medium and intermediate-
>   range ballistic warheads . . . . around 1,000
> Medium-range bombers, number of
>   warheads . . . . 750 to 1,000
>   Total   3,049 to 3,580

In the early 1980s the USSR introduced new classes of surface ships with substantial cruise missile capability, as well as substantial munitions storage capability, which would provide for reloads. This increased the values for the Northern Fleet substantially, perhaps by 25 percent or more, but probably did not alter the values for the Baltic at all because these ships were not deployed in the Baltic.

40. Harald Hamrin, "Soviet Experts on Scandinavia: We Are Ready to Negotiate on a Nuclear Weapon-Free Zone," *DN*, October 29, 1985.

41. Bobo Scheutz, "Soviet Admiral: Doubts That Submarines Had Violated Swedish Waters," *SvD*, May 13, 1984. In February 1986, Admiral Vladimir Chernavin, head of the Soviet navy, commented in an interview to the Soviet paper *Moskovskije Novosti* that the Swedish allegations, commissions, and investigations were a "circus intended for a dreary naiveté. . . . As commander in chief of the Soviet Fleet, I declare in the most serious way: not a single one of our boats is to be found in Norway's or Sweden's territorial waters." "Soviet Naval Chief: There are No Submarines Off Sweden's Coast," *DN*, February 20, 1986.

42. Mats Segfors, "Marshal Ogarkov's Uneasiness," *SvD*, May 6, 1984.

43. Norwegian Ministry of Defense, "Analysis of Operations in Sunnhordland, April 27–May 6, 1983," p. 3.

44. "Norway: Charges of Spying Against Ikkevold," *DN*, April 29, 1985.

45. Jacob Borressen, "Foreign Submarines in Norwegian Territorial Waters?" *HHD*, no. 26 (March 12, 1984).

46. Johan J. Holst, "Coast States Defense Against Submarines in Peacetime," 7.

47. Johan Holst, "After the Submarine Hunt," *SvD*, May 6, 1983; Johan Holst, "The Lessons of the Submarine Episodes," *Aftenposten*, May 7, 1983.

48. Captain Nils Bruzelius, "Sweden's Territorial Sea: A Motorway for Submarines," *MN*, no. 5–6 (December 1982): 4–5. This was the Swedish publication that was extensively misused in various transformations in the Soviet disinformation campaign that followed the Hårsfjärden events.

49. Colonel Jonathan Alford, "The Northern Flank as Part of Europe: Some Thoughts on Nordic Security," The Royal Academy of War Science, *Handlingar Och Tidskrift* 188, no. 6 (1984): 299–307. See also Harald Hamrin, "British Researcher on the Submarine Violations: USSR Wants to Weaken Swedish Air Force," *DN*, December 10, 1984.

50. The Swedish air force has nevertheless suffered serious losses in capability, but for entirely unrelated reasons that have affected the Danish air force as well. In the first four months of

1986 alone, 40 Swedish air force pilots left military service and another 40 were seeking to do the same. Because of the difference in pay, they sought employment in the civilian airline sector. The percentage of total pilots in the Swedish air force that have sought alternative employment in this manner is quite significant. See *SvD*, September 25, 1985, October 22, 1985, and November 24, 1985; *DN*, January 19, 1986, February 1, 1986, April 3, 6, and 9, 1986.

51. Claes Löfgren, "Defense Weakened," 7 *Dagar*, February 24, 1984.

52. Ingmar Oldberg, "Peace Campaign and Submarines: Soviet Policy Towards Sweden," *Världspolitikens Dagsfrågor*, no. 11 (Stockholm: Swedish Institute of International Affairs, 1982), 20–30.

53. Liberal Party Working Group, "Sweden and Submarine Incidents: A Security and Military Policy Perspective," *Folkpartiet Informerar 1983*, September 15, 1983.

54. Carl Bildt, "Soviet Poses Political Demands," *SvD*, May 7, 1984; Andres Kung and Jörgen Weibull, "The USSR and Our Foreign Policy Debate: Demands Our Adjustment," *SvD*, May 26, 1984.

There was one other suggestion that apparently was discussed privately in Finland but that has never been reported in the Swedish press – that "The USSR was playing 1939 again." This description was provided by an older Finnish researcher and government adviser who remembered the events of 1939. In 1939, the Soviet government made explicit demands on Finland. The USSR argued that, jointly, Finland and Estonia could block the exit of the Soviet fleet from Leningrad and asked for the Finnish base at Hankö and to be allowed to base Soviet troops in Finland. Finland refused.

In this environment, the USSR sent aircraft over Finnish territory, apparently as far as Sweden. The aircraft were observed, and articles about them appeared in the Finnish press. They were referred to as the "mystery planes," and they were attributed as having been Soviet. The Soviet press took up the Finnish newspaper reports with the theme "capitalist Finland is accusing us unjustly." Afterward, Finnish interpreters assumed that the provocations were designed to stir Soviet public feelings against Finland as a support of the war to come. By analogy, this would imply that the submarine intrusions were a conscious effort to turn

Sweden virtually into an enemy. The analogue also requires a much more imminent war situation.

55. Alford, "The Northern Flank as Part of Europe: Some Thoughts on Nordic Security," 304–305.

56. Tomas Ries, "Soviet Submarines in Sweden: Psychological Warfare in the Region," *International Defense Review* 17, no. 6 (June 1984): 695–696.

57. The 1984 Parliamentary Committee, *Swedish Security Policy in the 1990s*, May 1, 1985, mimeographed, 111 pages.

58. Ibid., 54. *Izvestia* immediately criticized the statements of the Swedish government on May 15.

59. Johan Holst, "The Military Buildup in the High North: Potential Implications for Regional Stability, A Norwegian Perspective," *NUPI Notat*, no. 318 B (Norwegian Institute of International Affairs, April 1985), mimeographed, 9 pages.

60. The 1984 Parliamentary Committee, *Swedish Security Policy in the 1990s*, 51–52.

61. Christiansson and Magnergård, "The Navy Can Only Defend a Limited Portion of the Coast."

62. Defense Staff Information Section, *Commander in Chief's Submarine Defense Plan*.

63. Lars Christiansson, "Interview with A. Shevchenko: Strong Swedish Policy Could Stop Soviet Border Violations," *SvD*, June 30, 1985.

64. Johan Galtung, the well-known Norwegian peace researcher, picked up this idea and suggested with great certainty that the USSR was seeking hiding places in Swedish waters for its newest SSN-18 SLBMs. This is not believable. The submarines carrying these missiles have never been seen in the Baltic and are much too large to permit inshore operations. Cecilia Steen-Johnsson, "Galtung on the Submarines: USSR Seeks Hiding Places," *DN*, November 16, 1985.

65. On October 8, 1983.

66. The Whisky-class submarines often leave the Baltic to take up patrols in the area west of Great Britain. Because Soviet ships including submarines carry standard ordnance on patrols, they could not go back to Leningrad in a crisis to load up with tactical nuclear weapons. This would presumably explain the presence of a nuclear torpedo on board the U-137 that was stranded in Sweden.

67. Dale R. Herspring, "GDR Naval Buildup," *Problems of Communism* 33, no. 1 (January–February 1984): 55–57 in particular. The original article is by Captain G. Poschel, "On Command of the Sea," *Militärwesen*, parts I-III, in the issues of May, June, and August 1982.

68. James T. Westwood, "Soviet Naval Theatre Forces: Their Strategy and Deployment," October 23, 1978, mimeographed, 37 pages.

In several recent studies, Peterson translates TVD into "theater of strategic military action (TSMA)" to make the phrase more meaningful to Western readers. Some authors, such as Michael MccGwire, also use "Okeanskiy TVD" instead of "Morskoy TVD" for the "MTV" or "maritime" TVD. Thus OTVD and MTVD are the same thing.

69. John G. Hines and Phillip A. Petersen, "Changing the Soviet System of Control: Focus on Theatre Warfare," *International Defense Review*, no. 3 (March 1986): 281–289; Phillip A. Petersen, *The Soviet Conceptual Framework for the Development and Application of Military Power*, 1984, mimeographed, 61 pages; U.S. Department of Defense, *Soviet Military Power 1986*, March 1986, pp. 11–12, 59–63.

70. *Soviet Military Encyclopedia*, vol. 2 (Moscow: Military Publishing House, 1976), 235.

71. Westwood, "Soviet Naval Theatre Forces," 9.

72. USSR General Staff Academy, *Dictionary of Basic Military Terms*, 1965, quoted in Westwood, "Soviet Naval Theatre Forces," 27.

73. Michael MccGwire, "Focus: Sweden and the Soviet Subs," transcript, Voice of America broadcast, May 3, 1984, mimeographed, 9 pages.

74. Michael MccGwire, *Military Objectives in Soviet Foreign Policy* (Washington, D.C.: The Brookings Institution, 1987).

75. Ibid.

76. U.S. Department of Defense, *Soviet Military Power*, 11–12, 59–63.

77. Hines and Petersen, "Changing the Soviet System of Control: Focus on Theatre Warfare," 284.

78. Michael MccGwire, "Soviet Military Objectives: Their Implications for War at Sea," in *Military Objectives in Soviet Foreign Policy*, 149, 468.

79. Erik Magnusson, "Norwegian Sea: Growing Unrest over the Soviet Fleet," *DN*, April 27, 1986.

80. V. E. Shlapentokh, "Moscow's War Propaganda and Soviet Public Opinion," *Problems of Communism* 33, no. 5 (September–October 1984): 88–94.

81. Phillip A. Petersen and John G. Hines, "The Conventional Offensive in Soviet Theater Strategy," *Orbis* 27, no. 3 (Fall 1983): 695–739.

82. *Fredsfakta*, no. 1, 1984, p. 9.

83. Ola Tunander, "The Sea is Scandinavia's Problem," *DN*, February 20, 1986. Tunander makes the major error of attributing the Reagan administration's proposals for "horizontal association" to Harold Brown and the Carter administration. See also Carl Bildt, "New Demands on Defense Policy," *DN*, April 4, 1986.

84. Colonel Bo Hugemark, "Soviet Spying Natural," *DN*, February 5, 1986.

85. Lars Christiansson, "Commander in Chief Denies Submarine Reports," *SvD*, June 23, 1985.

86. Charles Petersen and Don Hinricksen, "Focus: Sweden and the Soviet Subs," VOA Broadcast.

87. Berner, *The USSR and the Nordic States: Cooperation, Security, and Conflicts During Fifty Years*, 115.

88. Robert G. Weinland, "The Soviet Naval Buildup in the High North – A Reassessment," paper from Conference on Nordic Security, The Center for International Affairs, Harvard University, April 19–20, 1985, mimeographed, 35 pages.

89. C. S. Northedge, ed., *The Use of Force in International Relations* (London: Faber and Faber, Ltd., 1974), 29.

Index